T4-AFY-437

WITHDRAWN

WITHDRAWN

NATO AFTER 2000

The NATO logo.

NATO AFTER 2000

THE FUTURE OF THE
EURO-ATLANTIC ALLIANCE

JOHN BORAWSKI AND
THOMAS-DURELL YOUNG

PRAEGER

Westport, Connecticut
London

Library of Congress Cataloging-in-Publication Data

Borawski, John, 1957–2000.
    NATO after 2000 : the future of the Euro-Atlantic Alliance / John Borawski and
Thomas-Durell Young.
      p. cm.
    Includes bibliographical references and index.
    ISBN 0–275–97179–1 (alk. paper)
    1. North Atlantic Treaty Organization.   2. World Politics—1989– I. Young,
Thomas-Durell. II. Title.
    UA646.3.B567   2001
    355′.031091821—dc21   00–061126

British Library Cataloguing in Publication Data is available.

Copyright © 2001 by the Estate of John Borawski and Thomas-Durell Young

All rights reserved. No portion of this book may be
reproduced, by any process or technique, without the
express written consent of the publisher.

Library of Congress Catalog Card Number: 00–061126
ISBN: 0–275–97179–1

First published in 2001

Praeger Publishers, 88 Post Road West, Westport, CT 06881
An imprint of Greenwood Publishing Group, Inc.
www.praeger.com

Printed in the United States of America

The paper used in this book complies with the
Permanent Paper Standard issued by the National
Information Standards Organization (Z39.48–1984).

10 9 8 7 6 5 4 3 2 1

In memoriam
John Borawski
25 August 1957 to 14 November 2000

For Mishka, Adrien, and Julien
in hopes that their generation is blessed with a better peace

CONTENTS

.

PREFACE

The North Atlantic Treaty Organization (NATO) celebrated its fiftieth anniversary in 1999. Regarded by its now nineteen member states as the bedrock of European security and the anchor for maintaining the transatlantic political and military bridge, the alliance continues to perform its "core function" of providing collective defense to its members.

But NATO has always been and is more than a defensive alliance. During the last decade of the last millennium, NATO proved able to promote democratic peace outside its treaty area by reaching out to its former adversaries during the cold war to assist them in bolstering their democratic transition and providing forces capable of working with NATO, and by deploying its tested assets in dynamic crisis management to check crimes against humanity and regional instability. As the only functioning security and political organization in Europe, NATO has demonstrated its ability to adapt to the new environment and continues to serve as a linchpin of the three U.S. national security core objectives: enhancing American security, bolstering economic prosperity, and promoting democracy and human rights abroad.

However, as NATO enters the 21st century and the third millennium, it will confront numerous challenges requiring urgent attention:

- *Command arrangements, force structures, and defense priorities will need to be reviewed.* They must conform less to national and allied politics than to military exigency. Congress must insist that the U.S. administration provide meaningful, regular progress reports specifically geared to the requirements of the Defense Capabilities Initiative.

- *Europe must do more, with more resources, and within, not outside, the alliance.* A credible, independent European defense identity is a myth, whereas European declaratory aspirations for a robust defense identity "separable but not separate" from NATO remain just that. It is only when the non-U.S. Allies correct key deficiencies in mobility, communications, and sustainability and augment defense budgets where necessary that Washington should review how key NATO responsibilities are allotted among nations. Ending the long delay in implementing the Combined Joint Task Force concept and concluding a NATO-EU (European Union) coordination agreement are priorities. In an era of restrained U.S. resources and growing overseas commitments, Washington must accept that shared responsibilities means shared decision making. Europe must comprehend that the United States requires a reliable and credible partner.

- *NATO may be failing in its core collective defense function* in the delusion that arms control by itself will contain the threat or use of weapons of mass destruction (WMD). Allied inability to address this threat collectively risks public support for NATO and a dangerous lowering of the nuclear threshold should NATO conventional forces fail to prevent or limit attack.

- *The legal justification should be clarified for NATO operations outside the treaty area* if there is an obstacle in the UN Security Council. Governments, parliaments, and the electorate must achieve a new understanding of "what price honor" and "call of duty." The principle of humanitarian intervention should be elaborated in the Organization for Security and Cooperation in Europe (OSCE).

- *The NATO-Russia relationship needs a jump start.* It requires a more imaginative approach to cooperation in conflict prevention and crisis management by way of joint operations, units, and defense capabilities. If Russia is, as NATO declares, no longer considered a potential enemy, then the relationship should fully reflect the spirit and substance of partnership.

- *NATO enlargement is riddled with contradictions* as to purpose, the role of geography, timing, and criteria. The dynamics of enlargement after the 1999 entry into NATO of the Czech Republic, Hungary, and Poland are flat. There is no reason to link an invitation with admission through arbitrary time scales or on factors other than the merits of the individual candidate. The NATO "Membership Action Plan" must not be allowed to become a delaying device.

- *The purposes of, and relationship between, the forty-five-state Euro-Atlantic Partnership Council and the fifty-four-state OSCE needs new thinking* to avoid duplication, paralysis, and bureaucratic sterility. Nations should have a *choice* of organizational responses to security challenges and an *equal sense of participation* in building European security. The United States should not obstruct other organizations from developing their potential vibrancy and relevance because of undue concerns of undermining the alliance.

This volume explores these issues in detail, and counsels that whoever sits in the White House in 2001 and beyond will hold a special responsibility to nurture the indispensable U.S. leadership of the alliance to ensure NATO's relevance to its own members and to Europe as a whole in the overriding interests of arriving at a better peace.

We are indebted to James R. Dunton, who served as imprint advisor and a source of constant encouragement, and to Dr. James T. Sabin, director, academic research and development, David Wilfinger, product manager, Andrew Hudak, production editor, and Fran Lyon, copy editor, at the Greenwood Publishing Group, for their tremendous assistance in the preparation of this volume. We also wish to thank for their support Bruce George, M.P., Ambassador Aleksi Härkönen, Károly Banai, and Captain Heinz Dieter Jopp, Bundesmarine.

ABBREVIATIONS

ABM	Anti-Ballistic Missile
ACE	Allied Command Europe
ACTORD	Activation Order
ACTWARN	Activation Warning
AMF	Allied Mobile Force
AN	Antonov (Aircraft)
ARRC	ACE Rapid Reaction Corps
AWACS	Airborne Early Warning and Control System
BENELUX	Belgium, Netherlands, Luxembourg
BMD	Ballistic Missile Defense
CEE	Central and Eastern Europe
CENTRAZBAT	Central Asian Battalion
CESDP	Common European Security and Defense Policy
CFE	Conventional Forces in Europe
CFSP	Common Foreign and Security Policy
CHODS	Chiefs of Defense Staff
CiO	Chairman-in-Office
CIS	Commonwealth of Independent States
CJTF	Combined Joint Task Force

CMX	Crisis Management Exercise
CR-CAST	Central Region-Chiefs of Army Staff
CRISEX	Crisis Exercise
CSBM	Confidence- and Security-Building Measure
CSCE	Conference on Security and Cooperation in Europe
CSS	Combat Service Support
DCI	Defense Capabilities Initiative
DIA	Defense Intelligence Agency
DSACEUR	Deputy Supreme Allied Commander, Europe
EADRCC	Euro-Atlantic Disaster Response Coordination Center
EAPC	Euro-Atlantic Partnership Council
EMOP	Enhanced and More Operational Partnership
ESDI	European Security and Defense Identity
EU	European Union
EUROCORPS	European Corps
EUROFOR	European Rapid Operational Force
FAWEU	Forces Answerable to the Western European Union
FRY	Federal Republic of Yugoslavia
FYROM	Former Yugoslav Republic of Macedonia
GDP	Gross Domestic Product
GUUAM	Georgia, Ukraine, Uzbekistan, Azerbaijan, Moldova
HLSG	High-Level Steering Group
HQ	Headquarters
IAEA	International Atomic Energy Agency
ICTY	International Criminal Tribunal for the Former Yugoslavia
IFI	International Financial Institution
IFOR	Implementation Force
INTEX	International Warning and Detection Exercise
IPP	Individual Partnership Program
JCS	Joint Chiefs of Staff
JSRC	Joint Subregional Command
KFOR	Kosovo Force
KVM	Kosovo Verification Mission

LANDCENT	Allied Land Forces Central Europe
LANDJUT	Allied Land Forces Schleswig-Holstein
LTDP	Long-Term Defense Plan
L-TS	Long-Term Study
MAD	Mutual Assured Destruction
MAP	Membership Action Plan
MC	Military Committee
MiG	Mikoyan-gurevich (aircraft)
MJLC	Multinational Joint Logistics Center
MNC	Major NATO Command
MPFSEE	Multinational Peacekeeping Force Southeastern Europe
MSC	Major Subordinate Command
MTW	Major Theater War
NAC	North Atlantic Council
NACC	North Atlantic Cooperation Council
NATO	North Atlantic Treaty Organization
NBC	Nuclear, Biological, Chemical
NGO	Non-Governmental Organization
NIS	Newly Independent States
NMD	National Missile Defense
NUC	NATO-Ukraine Commission
OOTW	Operations Other than War
OPCOM	Operational Command
OPCON	Operational Control
OSCE	Organization for Security and Cooperation in Europe
PFP	Partnership for Peace
PGM	Precision-Guided Munition
PJC	Permanent Joint Council
PSC	Principal Subordinate Command
PSO	Peace Support Operation
SACEUR	Supreme Allied Commander, Europe (also Strategic Commander, Europe)
SECI	Southeast European Cooperation Initiative
SEDM	Southeast Europe Defense Ministerial

SEEI	Southeast Europe Initiative
SFOR	Stabilization Force
SHAPE	Supreme Headquarters Allied Powers Europe
SOFA	Status of Forces Agreement
SPP	State Partnership Program
SSC	Smaller-scale Contingency
STANAG	Standardization Agreement
TOA	Transfer of Authority
UN	United Nations
UNGA	UN General Assembly
UNHCR	UN High Commissioner for Refugees
UNMIK	UN Mission (Interim Administration) in Kosovo
UNPREDEP	UN Preventive Deployment Force
UNPROFOR	UN Protection Force
UNSC	UN Security Council
UNSCR	UNSC Resolution
WEU	Western European Union
WMD	Weapons of Mass Destruction
WMDI	WMD Initiative
XFOR	Extraction Force

INTRODUCTION

Fifty years after NATO's creation, the destinies of North America and Europe remain inseparable. When we act together, we safeguard our freedom and security and enhance stability more effectively than any of us could alone. Now, and for the century about to begin, we declare as the fundamental objectives of this Alliance enduring peace, security and liberty for all people of Europe and North America.

> NATO Washington Declaration
> April 23, 1999

U.S. defense efforts in Europe are aimed at achieving a peaceful, stable region where an enlarged NATO, through U.S. leadership, remains the preeminent security organization for promoting stability and security. Further, the United States seeks positive and cooperative Russian-NATO and Ukrainian-NATO relations and strengthened relations with Central and Eastern European nations outside of NATO. The United States desires a region in which all parties peacefully resolve their religious, political, and ethnic tensions through existing security structures and mechanisms. The United States and European nations should also work together to counter drug trafficking, terrorism, and the proliferation of NBC weapons and associated delivery systems. . . . The broad demands of the strategy require a full array of military capabilities . . . of sufficient size and scope to meet the most demanding missions, including defeating large-scale, cross-border aggression in two theaters nearly simultaneously, conducting the full range of

smaller-scale contingency (SSC) operations, and supporting routine
shaping activities.

William S. Cohen, Secretary of Defense
Annual Report to the President and the Congress
February 2000

Three months after the Warsaw Pact dissolved in July 1991, and two
months before the Soviet Union expired in December of the same year,
NATO Secretary General Manfred Wörner predicted that NATO would become "the core security organization of a future Euro-Atlantic architecture
in which all states, irrespective of their size or geographical location, must
enjoy the same freedom."[1] An alliance formed in 1949, four years after the
end of World War II, to reintegrate defeated Germany into the Western
mainstream, deter and defend against possible aggression or intimidation
by the Soviet Union, and formally link the United States and Europe, could
now serve as the foundation of a new security system not only for its members, but for the whole of Europe.

For most of NATO's existence, a basic tenet had been that "The United
States cannot counter this Soviet threat by itself. To maintain a strong conventional deterrent, therefore, we participate in a collective defense that in-
corporates the strength of our allies in the defense of our mutual interest."[2]
Yet, when that identifiable threat vanished beyond all expectations, NATO
moved beyond containment to help reshape the strategic environment itself on democratic lines as the best hope for stability.

True, President Woodrow Wilson had evoked similar thoughts in his
"Fourteen Points" of January 1918 regarding international guarantees of
political independence and territorial integrity "to great and small nations
alike" (although also calling for the "autonomous development" of peoples). His liberal vision was only to be bloodstained beyond the imagination of the generations of the pre-World War II years by powerful members
of the League of Nations and later the United Nations. "Realists" could
only be reinforced in their skepticism of the usefulness of organizations in
promoting peaceful settlement of disputes as advocated by "Neoliberals."

And yet, perhaps the change of truly Copernican proportions in
East-West relations beginning with Presidents Ronald Reagan and Mikhail
Gorbachev, and spearheaded by regime opponents Vaclav Havel in
Czechoslovakia and Lech Walesa in Poland, had made the time ripe for
shaping a civilized Europe free from fear and want among new and old democracies alike. And, if so, NATO could prove a prime contractor for security and stability.

Life itself has in part borne out Wörner's vision. NATO defied those on
both sides of the Atlantic who advocated bringing NATO to the gallows
pole, withdrawing U.S. forces from Europe, compelling Western Europe to
look after its own defense, preserving a divided Germany, or substituting

NATO for a pan-European security arrangement including Russia.[3] George Washington had cautioned the nation in 1796 against "permanent alliances, with any portion of the foreign world," and Thomas Jefferson warned of "entangling and embroiling our affairs with those of Europe." Yet, NATO persevered because it alone provided a credible collective defense umbrella that remains the fundament of its members' national security, a politico-military bridge between North America and Europe—each being the other's largest trading and investment partner on the order of trillions of dollars and of more than six million jobs on each side of the Atlantic. NATO was able to adapt to conduct crisis management outside its treaty area while building partner relations with all countries of Europe, and underpinned each of the three core U.S. national security objectives: enhancing American security; bolstering U.S. economic prosperity; and promoting democracy and human rights.[4] And despite a Congress skeptical of foreign commitments and doubts about whether the allies are doing their "fair share," NATO still enjoys the support of the House and Senate. The U.S. Senate, acting upon the disastrous lessons of World War II, endorsed on June 11, 1948 the Vandenburg Resolution supporting: "Association of the United States, by constitutional process, with such regional and other collective arrangements as are based on continuous and effective self-help and mutual aid, and as affect its national security."

Of course, the 21st century will not be like the first five decades of NATO's existence. Europe has recovered. Germany is united and at peace with all of its neighbors. The United States is no less intensively engaged in foreign commitments than during the cold war. In such circumstances, Henry Kissinger has suggested that "When there is no longer a single threat and each country perceives its perils from its own national perspective, those societies which had nestled under American protection will feel compelled to assume greater responsibility for their own security."[5] However, greater responsibility sharing by Europe is exactly what both Washington and its allies seek to accomplish, but *through* NATO and not duplicative of it. And even after the passing of five decades and Europe's emergence as the largest economic and monetary area in the world apart from the United States, *both* North America and Europe remain jointly dedicated to preserving NATO's "core function" of the collective defense of its present nineteen members, as set down in Article 5 of the founding Washington Treaty of April 4, 1949, which the Senate approved by an 83:13 vote:

The Parties agree that an armed attack against one or more of them in Europe or North America shall be considered an attack against them all, and consequently they agree that, if such an armed attack occurs, each of them, in exercise of the right of individual or collective self-defense recognized by Article 51 of the Charter of the United Nations, will assist the Party or Parties so attacked by taking forthwith, individually, and in concert with the other Parties, such action *as it deems necessary, in-*

cluding the use of armed force, to restore and maintain the security of the North Atlantic area [emphasis added].

Even in the absence of an identifiable threat, collective defense *is* what current and aspiring members want as the basis of their national security, and with the aspiration that NATO can do for the rest of Europe what it did for Western Europe—what President Harry S Truman stated on March 12, 1947 as the imperative of assisting "free peoples to work out their own destinies in their own way." The integrated military structure and habits of multinational cooperation not only make possible effective military operations across the spectrum, but support important and still relevant political goals:

- preventing destabilizing "renationalization" of defense and nuclear proliferation
- enhancing transparency
- reinforcing shared security and political interests
- preventing disputes between members—even imperfect democracies—from escalating
- strengthening the transatlantic politico-military bridge

When the United States chooses or is compelled to act without the alliance in non-Article Five operations, NATO provides the infrastructure—U.S. and allied installations commonly funded in Europe—for campaigns such as Desert Storm against Iraq in 1991, Provide Comfort, the continuing surveillance of safe havens in Iraq for Kurds in the North, and Southern Watch, for the "Marsh Arabs" in the South. Indeed, the NATO Strategic Commander, Europe (SACEUR), is always also the Commander-in-Chief of the U.S. European Command with headquarters (HQ) in Stuttgart.

As the only functioning security organization, NATO can also provide the resources—intelligence, communications, strategic lift, facilities—to "coalitions of the willing" of NATO and non-NATO states alike to address risks to security and affronts to humanity within or outside Europe.

At the NATO fiftieth anniversary summit in Washington on April 23 and 24, 1999, the allies declared as their fundamental objectives "enduring peace, security and liberty for all people of Europe and North America." The NATO Secretary General, Lord Robertson of Port Ellen, has described NATO as remaining "at the center of European security, with new missions, new members, and ever-deepening partnerships." He sees his priorities as sixfold:

- more effective and interoperable forces, with the Kosovo crisis having proved "a wake-up call" as well as a success
- a "more mature" transatlantic security relationship with the European Security and Defense Identity having become "an urgent necessity" and "no longer just an attractive idea" to create "a more balanced Alliance, with a stronger European input"
- a stronger relationship with Russia, with security in the Euro-Atlantic area working best when NATO and Russia work together from peace-keeping to nuclear safety to arms control
- lasting peace and stability in the Balkans, including preparing states in the region for NATO membership
- strengthened links between NATO and Ukraine and with other Partners including giving Partners more say in planning and conducting NATO-led peace support operations
- preparing NATO for the next round of enlargement.[6]

Yet, nothing should be taken for granted. The new millennium may well continue a trend of possible U.S. global unilateralism, selective engagement, or isolationism. The U.S. Congress is less versed in international affairs than ever before. Europe seeks to react to America's singular superpower status by purporting to strengthen its own defense as well as political identity, and the relationship between new European structures and NATO remains to be solidified and in a sensible way. Russia's destiny remains a matter of speculation. NATO may confront direct challenges from "nontraditional" sources from the alliance perspective, such as international terrorism, uncontrolled migration, the disintegration of states, and proliferation of weapons of mass destruction. Security must be understood beyond the military dimensions alone but in comprehensive terms, encompassing political, economic, and human dimensions, and will require active leadership.

Consequently, whoever sits in the White House in 2001 and thereafter will need to reinforce the perpetual truth that the surest means to hold NATO together and sustain allied efforts for democratic peace is U.S. leadership. And they will bear a heavy responsibility to advance what is probably the most important U.S. foreign policy achievement, although still a work in progress, of the 1990s: the transformation of NATO from an alliance focused on static defense against a vanished clear and present danger to a security and political organization projecting its values and capabilities in the interests of the whole of Europe, eroding the dividing of the past, and endeavoring to prevent new ones from arising.

This volume critically explores the key issues before NATO as it enters the 21st century through the prism of the U.S. "Triple Crown" strategy for engaging Europe through NATO, the Organization for Security and Cooperation in Europe (OSCE), and the European Union (EU). Chapter 1 critically examines how the alliance is attempting to develop capabilities and command and force structures to perform the full range of NATO missions. Chapter 2 explores the prospects for a better transatlantic balance of responsibility taking account EU aspirations to a common defense policy. Chapter 3 assesses the legal basis for NATO missions outside the treaty area when the UN Security Council (UNSC) fails to act, drawing on the 1999 NATO air campaign against Serbia-Montenegro, and asks how allies understand the question of what is worth sending armed forces into harm's way. Chapters 4, 5, and 6 inquire into NATO's external adaptation through its special relationship with Russia, enlargement, and outreach to all European and other states. Chapter 7 then looks at the prospects for a more inclusive security system in which all North American and European states have an equal voice. It is intended for politicians, diplomats, officials, the military, academics, students, and all those sharing the vision of a better peace and working to prevent it from once again disappearing into infinity.

RISKS AND CAPABILITIES

Our experience in Bosnia has been a significant success in both human-itarian and geopolitical terms, but it also revealed that NATO's trans-formation from a fixed, positional defense to a flexible, mobile defense is incomplete.... To merely maintain a force designed to defend against Warsaw Pact aggression, or to make only superficial adjustments, would be a serious dereliction of our duty to our soldiers, our nations, our alliance, and our future.[1]

U.S. Secretary of Defense William Cohen
November 13, 1998

We have gone beyond collective defense to develop new tools for help-ing our partners build their own stability and help us defend our com-mon values.[2]

U.S. NATO Ambassador Alexander Vershbow
May 11, 2000

SECURITY CHALLENGES

Although NATO grew from the 1948 Brussels Treaty among the Benelux countries, France, and the United Kingdom and intended in part to prevent "a renewal by Germany of an aggressive policy," the Washington Treaty identifies no enemy. Its broad and enduring *raison d'être* is nothing less than achieving the primary purpose of the UN—the maintenance of interna-tional peace and security—and "to safeguard the freedom, common heritage and civilization of their peoples, founded on the principles of democracy, individual liberty and the rule of law." For most of its history, NATO was compelled to plan on the assumption "That the USSR will attempt to defeat the forces of the North Atlantic Treaty nations and reach the Atlantic Seaboard, the Mediterranean and the Middle East,"[3] and that NATO's mission was to defeat this offensive and maintain the ability to undertake strategic bombing by "all means possible"—with the United States relying heavily on its atomic and then thermonuclear advantage to compensate for what it portrayed as a tremendous Soviet conventional force advantage. The current 1999 NATO Strategic Concept not so obliquely acknowledges as a security "challenge" and "risk" "the existence of powerful nuclear forces outside the Alliance" which NATO "has to take into account if security and stability in the Euro-Atlantic area are to be maintained" (see paragrah 21 in Appendix A). In the view of the U.S. Department of Defense:

Russia could, in the coming years, reestablish its capability to project large-scale offensive military forces along its periphery . . . Should Russia's political system fail to stabilize over the longer term, disintegration of Russia as a coherent state could pose major security challenges for the United States and the international community.[4]

However, the Pentagon affirms that the United States faces no global rival today, and is unlikely to face one "through at least 2015."[5] NATO's current Strategic Concept also recognizes, as did the earlier 1991 version, that the past threat of large-scale aggression against NATO is highly unlikely, and Russia is no longer regarded as an enemy. The reference in the 1991 Strategic Concept to NATO preserving "the strategic balance within Europe" with specific reference to "Soviet military capability and build-up potential" has been abandoned, although the new concept states that the threat of "large scale conventional aggression" emerging over the "longer term" exists (see paragraph 20 in Appendix A).

The chairman of the NATO Military Committee, Admiral Guido Venturoni, has described the new Concept as recognizing "that maintaining a strategic balance is no longer paramount in the current security environment," exists and that "we will continue to move away from the old planning tools of strategic parity [although still maintained for purposes of U.S.-Russia strategic nuclear arms control, disregarding other nuclear powers declared and undeclared], concentrating instead on the functional characteristics [e.g., command and control, logistics] and 'sufficiency' in military force needed for credible deterrence and timely and effective crisis management."[6] NATO's most likely challenges today are multidirectional, multifaceted, and often unpredictable or not recognized at an early stage, such as regional crises at the periphery of the alliance caused by ethnic strife, territorial disputes, quests for self-determination, disruption of vital resources, and the threat or use of weapons of mass destruction (WMD) by states or nonstate actors.

Some of these risks may directly affect the security of a NATO member, and should it lead to an attack upon it, Article 5 would come into play. However, Article 5 is not, as is sometimes assumed, an automatic trigger to go to war, as Pat Buchanan suggests in arguing for amending the NATO treaty "so that involvement in future European wars is an option, not a certainty."[7] To the contrary, as Secretary of State Dean Acheson noted during the negotiations leading up to the treaty, "no power on earth could force any other action upon any signatory," even though "decent people keep their contract obligations."[8] But these "contract obligations" are no more than what each ally deems necessary. As President Bill Clinton wrote on September 10, 1997, to U.S. Senators deliberating about NATO enlargement: Article 5 "does not define what actions would constitute 'an attack' or prejudge what Alliance decisions might then be made . . . members would need to exercise their judgment on a case-by-case basis in formulating the appropriate response."

But even short of an attack against an ally and with it the presumption—but not the certainty—that allies would respond collectively by all necessary means, Article 4 of the Washington Treaty specifically requires consultations in the event any member believes its political independence, territorial integrity, or "security" is threatened, with the Strategic Concept adding "coordination" of effort to "consultation." In June 1982 in Bonn, the North Atlantic Council (NAC) agreed that "All of us have an interest in peace and security in other regions of the world. . . . Those of us who are in a position to do so will endeavor to respond to requests for assistance from sovereign states whose security and independence is threatened."

Indeed, NATO's first live operation took place outside the treaty area with arguably no threat to Allied security, in former Yugoslavia through Operations Maritime Guard and then Sharp Guard (which challenged 74,000 merchant vessels in the Adriatic), Operation Deny Flight (NATO's first-ever shots in anger, on February 28, 1994), Operation Deliberate Force (the massive bombing from August to September 1995 against Bosnian Serb positions—NATO's largest military action in history at the time), followed by Implementation Force (IFOR), Stabilization Force (SFOR), Operation Allied Force, and Kosovo Force (KFOR) to avoid humanitarian catastrophe, wider destabilization of the region, and to demonstrate allied credibility. NATO not only conducted military operations through air strikes and operations other than war (OOTW) or peace support operations (PSOs). It also assumed humanitarian relief tasks normally associated with other organizations such as the UN and International Committee of the Red Cross, compelled in part by a need to avoid flooding NATO nations such as Germany with refugees as occurred during the Bosnian War, and foil President Slobodan Milosevic's attempt to destabilize Albania and the former Yugoslav Republic of Macedonia (FYROM, hereinafter Macedonia).

Thus, whether under Articles 4 or 5, NATO retains wide latitude in determining how and when to bring force to bear, recognizing that an Article 4 situation can escalate to an Article 5 emergency. Specifically, then chairman of the NATO Military Committee, General Klaus Naumann, identified in 1998 four broad risks the alliance had to take into account:

1. "stable instability" and "residual risk" in Russia
2. unresolved issues in Europe, as in the Balkans
3. challenges on the periphery of NATO, with the Mediterranean viewed as "NATO's most endangered region"
4. "new risks" (at least for NATO) such as cyber-warfare, destabilizing migrations, terrorism, and WMD to which the alliance concedes it has "no ready answers"[9]

And the U.S. Defense Intelligence Agency (DIA) estimates:

the turmoil and uncertainty that have characterized the post–Cold War era will last at least another decade . . . because most of the underlying factors remain in place—uneven economic and demographic development; disparities in wealth and resource distribution; continued ethnic, religious and cultural strife; broad, rapid technology advances and attendant proliferation of advanced weapons in certain regional and global security structures; international criminal activity with national security overtones; the continued existence of rogue, renegade and outlaw states, resistance to the rapid expansion of Western ideas and culture; natural disasters and environmental issues; and numerous critical uncertainties. . . . No condition, circumstance or power is likely to emerge over the next 10 to 20 years which will somehow transcend them and lead to a more stable global order.[10]

Indeed, during the transitional months from 1999 to 2000, it was emblematic of the complex security environment that:

- Renewed conflict in Chechnya risked spilling over not only into other Russian republics, but Georgia, and isolating Russia from the "international community."
- Concerns were expressed that supporting the autonomy of former Soviet republics such as in the energy-rich but turbulent Caspian Sea region and Caucasus could prove "the most important issue on the U.S.-Russian agenda in the coming decade."[11]
- The United States reinforced warnings that North Korea, Iraq, and Iran could acquire long-range WMD delivery means within a few years (although existing shorter-range missiles could already pose a threat to, for example, U.S. bases in Japan).

- China again resorted to brinksmanship by threatening that it would resolve the Taiwan question by force if sought-after negotiations on unification failed.

- The United States distributed 14,000 gas masks to its embassy employees and their dependents in South Korea in the event of a nerve gas, blister agent, or anthrax attack from the North (with the third largest army in the world and having completed its heaviest winter training cycle in recent years despite a horrific economic situation).

- Several hundred UN peacekeepers were held hostage by murderous rebels in Sierra Leone, whereas the UN was unsuccessful in preventing a flare-up of the border war between Ethiopia and Eritrea that had claimed perhaps as many as 70,000 lives over two years—another display of the organization's inability to make peace.

- Rhetoric about a harmonious multiethnic future for Serbia seemed as naïve as ever, with Serbian-Kosovar Albanian skirmishing continuing and de facto partitioning in play, despite the trappings of a cease-fire and the trading of "Kosovo Liberation Army" for "Kosovo Protection Corps" but with many of the same individuals, and with NATO nations failing to live up to their postconflict military and financial commitments. This prompted the director of the UN Interim Administration in Kosovo (UNMIK), Bernard Kouchner, to draw urgent attention to "an absurd, humiliating and self-defeating way to run anything, let alone a project that embodies the prestige of the United Nations"[12] (as the OSCE had initially experienced in Bosnia) and compelling NATO forces to undertake policing and other tasks for which they were not trained. Concurrently, Congress sought to set a July 2001 deadline for a withdrawal of U.S. troops absent the next administration receiving specific consent from legislators (defeated by only five votes on May 18, 2000)—even as the General Accounting Office reported that "all areas of the Balkans continue to face major unresolved political, social, and other problems that will contribute to regional instability over the next 5 years," such that "These problems also will require the continued security presence provided by NATO-led forces."[13]

- More than one million internally displaced persons and refugees were still at large as a result of the war in Bosnia, with the presidency still unable to assume full responsibility and undertake needed economic reforms, and with NATO continuing to evade the issue of capturing indicted war criminals with the absurd argument that this task was the primary responsibility of local authorities while acknowledging that those same authorities were protecting the indictees.

- Iranian leader Ayatollah Ali Khameini called for Israel's destruction as the "final solution" for a Middle East settlement.

- The U.S. Energy Information Administration could state no more than that it was "very unlikely" that a nuclear accident might result from a year 2000 Y2K problem at a Soviet-designed nuclear power plant.

- A Y2K "Center for Strategic Stability" was established at Peterson Air Force Base, Colorado, as a public diplomacy effort to demonstrate that both the United States and Russia were jointly monitoring any accidental missile launchings (to be absorbed by 2001 by a joint early warning center in Moscow, as agreed in 1997).

- The last weeks of 1999 witnessed the largest counter-terrorism effort in U.S. history.

What NATO is in the process of determining is how it could play a special role together with other organizations in meeting these challenges, viewing "security" in a comprehensive sense beyond collective defense alone.

Table 1-1
NATO's Fundamental Security Tasks

Security: To provide one of the indispensable foundations for a stable Euro-Atlantic security environment, based on the growth of democratic institutions and commitment to the peaceful resolution of disputes, in which no country would be able to intimidate or coerce any other through the threat or use of force.

Consultation: To serve, as provided for in Article 4 of the Washington Treaty, as an essential transatlantic forum for allied consultations on any issues that affect their vital interests, including possible developments posing risks for members' security, and for appropriate coordination of their efforts in fields of common concern.

Deterrence and Defense: To deter and defend against any threat of aggression against any NATO member state as provided for in Articles 5 and 6 of the Washington Treaty.

And in order to enhance the security and stability of the Euro-Atlantic area:

Crisis Management: To stand ready, case-by-case and by consensus, in conformity with Article 7 of the Washington Treaty [recognizing the primary responsibility of the UN Security Council (UNSC) for international peace and stability], to contribute to effective conflict prevention and to engage actively in crisis management, including crisis response operations.

Partnership: To promote wide-ranging partnership, cooperation, and dialogue with other countries in the Euro-Atlantic area, with the aim of increasing transparency, mutual confidence, and the capacity for joint action with the alliance.

Source: *The Alliance's Strategic Concept* (1999).

DEFENSE CAPABILITIES INITIATIVE

NATO's immediate task is to enhance interoperability across the board for both Article 4 and Article 5 missions. This may seem puzzling, as supposedly the NATO defense planning system and decades of multinational exercises were designed precisely to achieve the ability for different allied armies, air forces, and navies to work seamlessly together. However, in the past the strategic requirement was the need to move largely conscript forces into predetermined positions in NATO Europe for main defense against an attack from the East. Each nation provided its own logistics support, although also relying on common NATO facilities such as bases and pipelines. Interoperability was relatively limited, and the assumption was that a conflict would be relatively short whether or not it escalated into nuclear warfare.[14] The focus was on maintaining a "layer cake" of eight heavy national corps to defend the inner-German border, and integration occurred at the army group level. "NATO did not need to explore ways the better to effect cooperation in the politically sensitive areas of, for example, force training, operational doctrine, and logistics."[15] Multinationality was limited to the small "show the flag" ACE Mobile Force (AMF) and the Allied Land Forces Schleswig-Holstein and Jutland Corps (LANDJUT). Europe's interest was largely regional and, for some nations, ex-colonial, and national budgets substantially more devoted to quality of life than in the United States.

In contrast, America was preoccupied not only with European but international security. This has not changed, although the defense budget was not increased in real terms during the 1990s until the last year of the decade. Over the 1990s, U.S. overseas deployments increased by 300 percent, while the overall force was reduced by 30 percent. The United States has Status of Forces Agreements (SOFAs) today with fifty-three countries to protect the rights of nearly half a million U.S. personnel and dependents. Of the 247,000 U.S. forces deployed abroad, 111,000 are in or afloat near Europe, including the major elements of two army divisions, 2.3 fighter wings, one carrier battle group, and one amphibious ready group. The current pace of operations, together with inadequate housing, has and will have a major impact on service members and their families, and the services confront declining retention rates.

Following NATO's military offensive, Operation Allied Force over Serbia-Montenegro from March 24 to June 10, 1999, the disparities between U.S and non-U.S. NATO capabilities were brought into a brighter spotlight. Although non-U.S. allies provided the bulk of ground forces in former Yugoslavia, this capabilities gap hampered the operation and undermined both the "European pillar" of NATO and Europe's aspirations to have the option for autonomous military action.

NATO Europe accounts for the equivalent of 60 percent of U.S. defense spending, but less than a third of equipment purchases, a sixth of research and development, and has acquired only 10 percent of U.S. power projection capability. Lord Robertson has noted that "There are around two million people in European armies in uniform today, and yet the Europe; allies had to struggle to get 40,000 to go and serve in Kosovo."[16] Beyo this, both sides, seeking to protect their national industries, remain reluctant to at long last create a cost-effective and fair transatlantic defense market, and "The costs of inaction mount daily."[17]

This European, and Canadian, unwillingness to reorient and increase defense expenditures had a clear impact on interoperability, high-tech weaponry, and power projection during Allied Force and the accompanying troop movements to Albania and Macedonia. U.S. Deputy Secretary of State Strobe Talbott warned: "Many Americans are saying: never again should the United States have to fly the lion's share of the risky missions in a NATO operation and foot by far the largest bill."[18] U.S. aircraft flew 53 percent of the combat sorties, 62 percent of all sorties, constituted 69 percent of the 1,058 aircraft involved, and carried out the majority of all-weather, round-the-clock missions and strikes with precision-guided munitions (PGMs)—which experienced a sharp drawdown in U.S. stocks. Only Canada, France, and Britain had similar capabilities but deploying far fewer air-craft. Not all allied pilots could even communicate securely, identify "friend or foe," or refuel in the air. French Army Chief of Staff General Jean-Pierre Kelche conceded: "Without American support, we couldn't have done all that we did."[19] U.S. Secretary of Defense William Cohen and chairman of the Joint Chiefs of Staff (JCS), General Henry Shelton, reported that "U.S. forces could not have continued the intense campaign in Kosovo and, at the same time, been prepared to fight and win two major theater wars [MTWs]" citing Southwest Asia and North Korea, and *Such disparities in capabilities will seriously affect our ability to operate as an effective alliance over the long term.*[20]

Moreover, however a convenient political justification, among the reasons NATO cited for not opting to deploy ground forces in Serbia-Montenegro during the air campaign was that it would have taken "several weeks" to assemble an invasion force. Yet, NATO committed itself as long ago as 1991 to enhance rapid reaction. Although there was more than adequate "early warning" of the Kosovo crisis, which erupted a year before Allied Force and after nine years of simmering tensions which brought about a Conference on Security and Cooperation in Europe (CSCE) preventive diplomacy mission between 1992 and 1993 (Yugoslavia did not renew its mandate—another indicator), and despite the fact that NATO was looking at different intervention options, Secretary Cohen and JCS Chairman Shelton publicly acknowledged on October 14, 1999, that the Pentagon astonishingly did not have "standing plans" for moving forces to Kosovo, and that the evolving situation in Kosovo strained its ability to do so rapidly.

As a result, resources were strained, reserves had not been sufficiently activated, and parallel U.S. and NATO command and control procedures complicated operational planning and unity of command (for example, B-2 stealth bombers were not under NATO command and flew each sortie from and back to their home base in Missouri). A need was identified for Precision-Guided Munition (PGM), electronic warfare, search, intelligence, and reconnaissance, and strategic lift improvements—even though Kosovo was hardly a Major Theater War (MTW). It took seventeen days for Army AH-64A *Apache* helicopters to deploy to Albania as a possible supplement to the air campaign, but they were never used because of the premium placed on avoiding collateral damage and doubts about their survivability once over Serbia. Because of Kosovo and Bosnia, two of the army's ten divisions (the tenth Mountain in Fort Drum, New York, and the first Infantry in Wurzburg, Germany) received in late 1999 the lowest of four readiness grades because of their inability to be called up for an MTW. "Unfortunately," stated Senator James M. Inhofe, chairman of the Readiness Subcommittee of the Senate Armed Services Committee, "today we have a 10–division Army performing the workload of 14 divisions," describing this as the worst readiness problem in twenty years.[21] The Defense Department responded by noting that steps were being taken to use National Guard units more frequently to free up active units for their principal MTW missions and modifying readiness reporting procedures to better reflect division readiness for units with dual missions, for "now that we're faced with a continuum presence and small-scale contingencies, as well as the MTWs, we're having to go back and relook" the reporting system.[22]

The remedy for this circumstance cannot be left to business as usual. How is it that the Defense Intelligence Agency (DIA) recognizes the risks of smaller contingencies, which are the most likely triggers for NATO or coalition military engagement in Europe, and NATO guidance calls for one small collective defense contingency *plus* two simultaneous non-Article 5 operations, but the Defense Department seemed to regard them as a distraction from planning for the unlikely MTW contingency? Is it because the "The Army remains intellectually and structurally mired in the Cold War planning environment of preparation for large-scale, high-intensity conventional war against like adversaries, even though the United States has all but run out of such enemies at least for the time being?"[23] Or is the U.S. focus on MTWs entirely valid, and is it the Europeans who should take care of their own backyard, and who could not be relied upon to assist the United States in MTWs such as Desert Storm that affected European interests more than U.S. security (Europeans contributed a mere 6 percent of ground and air forces to Desert Storm)? Or would this division of labor lead to a two-tier alliance—a "bleeding" and a "precision" class?

Furthermore, what conceivable purpose apart from domestic politics, as imagined by the White House, was served by the administration declaring publicly that it would not send ground troops into a "non-permissive" environment? This was rightly viewed as "strategic folly" by commanders, whereby an air campaign was divorced from a "Hell on Wheels" option,[24] and a position which had to be reviewed at a late stage following the inconclusive air campaign. The United States also alternated between resorting to NATO and unilateral steps to achieve a negotiated settlement, and the key ingredients of surprise and deception went amiss as NATO announced the air campaign. According to press reports, Belgrade was even able to acquire NATO air tasking orders for several weeks, either because of espionage or negligence within NATO.[25]

As a result, although NATO achieved its limited politico-military objectives, military performance in NATO's first coalition war and the first in the "information age" seemed more like the improvisations of an ad hoc coalition than the performance of a well-honed military machine.

Was NATO still prone to the "superficial adjustments" of which Secretary Cohen warned?

What had been the cumulative value of thousands of NATO exercises in the 1990s?

What is the purpose of the NATO Force Goal system—which poses no more than "reasonable challenges" to nations—if the problems made manifest in Allied Force were identified by that system *several years ago*, and underscored in the prior IFOR/SFOR mission, but which nations failed to rectify?

Moreover, even given the MTW focus, it had taken six months to build up forces against Iraq and even then suffered from inefficiencies in types of units, supplies, and munitions. The ability of the allies to achieve their goal in both Desert Storm and Allied Force cannot obscure these military deficiencies and the fact that the adversary in those two campaigns was no match for the alliance.

Because likely future scenarios will require not static but rapidly deployable forces able to operate outside the treaty area, at the 1999 Washington Summit, a 1998 U.S.-proposed "Defense Capabilities Initiative" (DCI) was agreed in principle with five functional area objectives:

1. Deployability and Mobility
2. Sustainability and Logistics
3. Command, Control, and Communications
4. Effective Engagement (e.g., air defenses and PGMs)
5. Survivability and Infrastructure

A High-Level Steering Group (HLSG) was then established to effect priorities and coordinate and integrate the efforts of the numerous NATO committees and bodies involved. By early 2000, key NATO committees had been reorganized with a view towards fulfilling DCI objectives as among their highest priorities, and fifty-eight areas had been identified for improvement.

DCI is hardly breaking new ground. Limited progress had heretofore been made in large part because of the inability of the non-U.S. allies to find the necessary funding to modernize forces and an intrinsic complacency under U.S. protection. For example, a 1978 supposedly agreed NATO initiative termed the Long-Term Defense Program (LTDP) which intended to enhance readiness, reinforcement, mobilization, and maritime posture fell well short because the Canadians and Europeans were simply not willing to make the necessary financial commitments (a 3 percent real increase in defense spending was the target). And this was when Soviet soldiers daily surveilled NATO defenses across the inner-German border and were acquiring the ability, or Pentagon analysts believed, to launch a surprise attack and occupy Western Europe (confirmed by the recovery of military documents after the unification of Germany).

Given this past, and with Europe preoccupied with building on monetary union and enlargement, it is hardly surprising that as of early 2000, the Pentagon verdict was that "the information so far available does not provide a sufficiently comprehensive picture of national implementation activities." Although there were "hopeful signs of movement towards increased defense spending," and whereas France, Germany, and the Netherlands were making efforts in areas such as pooling civilian and military lift, nonetheless "unresponsive defense budgets continue to erode Alliance capabilities."[26]

For instance, Germany would need to spend an estimated $22 billion over ten years to adapt its forces, which are still largely geared toward main defense, but Chancellor Gerhard Schröder simultaneously sought a cut by half that amount by 2003 instead.[27] Germany spends only 1.5 percent of its Gross Domestic Product (GDP) on defense (versus 3.2, 2.8, and 2.3 percent for the United States, France, and the United Kingdom, respectively)—such that the *Luftwaffe* lacked inter alia its own aerial refueling capability in Allied Force which even the far smaller Netherlands possesses.

Some European officials have been, predictably, skeptical of the U.S. DCI initiative and have viewed it as not so subtle encouragement to buy American, such as radios and PGMs.[28] The United States asserts it favors a transatlantic approach and recognizes that there are steps needed to be taken to make that approach versus a "buy Europe" one more attractive, namely open markets and reasonable technology nontransfer rules. In May 2000 the Clinton administration launched a "Defense Trade Security Initiative" pledging to expedite review of export licenses and streamline export controls with allies.

Moreover, in the absence of an identifiable threat, force planning is hardly obvious: should an ally maintain a ready battalion, brigade, or division for Operations other than War (OOTW)? The point of an alliance is precisely to *share* the burden, but that sharing resists any "one-size-fits-all approach" and Washington is not insisting on identical capabilities for each ally, but rather only compatible ones. There has never been a consensus within the alliance on burden sharing and there is no reason to expect this will change, leaving open questions either side can raise:

- Does Belgium need an aircraft carrier, or does its comparative advantage in mine hunting suffice?

- Should Iceland create armed forces, or is its geographic position along the transatlantic lines of communication itself a major and sufficient asset to NATO, even given the absence of a Soviet naval threat?

- How is the fact that the United States is at the bottom of the list of NATO nations in contributing foreign assistance, a form of conflict prevention, as a percentage of GDP, or the fact that Germany has been by far the largest contributor of assistance to Central and Eastern Europe (CEE) and the Newly Independent States (NIS) and hosts the largest number of U.S. bases in Europe, to be taken into account in the overall picture?

- Did the United States truly share its geostrategic burden by doing the minimum to assist Russia and then the NIS to make the (yet to be seen) great leap forward?

- If the geographical reach of likely NATO force projection is unknown, does an ally invest in C-130s or C-17s, or lease commercial aircraft and ships?

- Is there anything necessarily wrong with an alliance of different tier members, ranging from the ground forces (the "bleeding class") to the precision strikers, to wit the U.S. notion that after Allied Force the responsibility for peacekeeping should devolve primarily if not entirely on the Europeans if only to minimize the risk of harm to U.S. troops, as if they should be regarded as the china and not the bull in the shop? Or, is a defense union divided between peacekeepers and warriors fundamentally counterproductive and incompatible with the notion of Europe acting without the United States in a crisis?

- How does the "one for all and all for one" principle of Article 5 apply to non-Article 5 missions?

- Furthermore, the new emphasis on non-Article 5 missions does not by itself answer long-standing defense issues before policymakers; for example, German Defense Minister Rudolph Scharping stated the following regarding conscription:

I do not wish that Germany reaches a similar situation to Great Britain, where they are considering having certain youthful offenders serve out their sentences in the armed forces [although fugitives from justice historically found a place in the French Foreign Legion]. I would also not wish to experience what we have seen in France, where the abolishment of conscription and the reduction of the army has led to a 30 percent increase in cost with no corresponding increase in performance. We should make sure that armed forces in democracies represent the entire spectrum of society—its potential, its values [precisely the advice NATO is giving the new or emerging democracies in Central and Eastern Europe].[29]

At the same time, the Supreme Allied Commander, Europe (SACEUR) cautions:

It is time to halt the reduction of resources dedicated to defense—the so-called peace dividend—and face up to the reality that in this still dangerous world security never comes cheap . . . NATO even in post-Cold War Europe must maintain *real* warfighting capabilities: rapid reaction forces with deployable command and control; Alliance intelligence fusion; air-ground reconnaissance; all-weather, full-spectrum engagement capabilities; and interoperable, survivable, sustainable forces.[30]

That is, although it may be difficult politically to find the additional resources for defense, and balances must be struck among competing priorities, it is all the same necessary to spend more and more wisely if agreed NATO Force Goals are not to remain declaratory and the potential of the alliance unrealized. Noted French defense expert François Heisbourg believes that given the inability to-date of NATO's defense planning and review process to rehaul fundamentally bloated European cold war-era force structures, "The only option that carries enough political weight to address Europe's structural defense weaknesses is the broad-based, deep-rooted European Union. . . . NATO can help through the [DCI], but the crux of the problem is in Europe as such, not NATO"[31]—clearly an area to monitor such that EU and NATO defense planning do not go separate ways. At the same time, although it is common to warn against duplication, Europe must recognize that NATO may not agree to make certain assets available for a non-NATO-led operation.

That said, high-level direction and profile given to DCI might work to the advantage of the alliance. Attention by senior officials to the details governing traditionally contentious matters such as multinationality, crisis response, and logistics could provide the necessary initiative to overcome some of the obstacles that have bedeviled earlier reform efforts. It must also be noted that the DCI, if implemented, would reinforce not only the European Pillar of NATO and the European Security and Defense Identity (ESDI), but the Membership Action Plan (MAP) announced at the Washington Summit to assist candidate NATO members, thus investing in both current *and future* allies. And as the High-Level Steering Group (HLSG) will explore involving partners in NATO-led non-Article 5 operations, greater interoperability will allow for more effective, wider coalition activity.

WEAPONS OF MASS DESTRUCTION

At the January 1994 Brussels Summit, the allies decided to "intensify and expand NATO's political and defense effort against proliferation" of

Weapons of Mass Destruction (WMD). The result was cosmetic. Committees but not hardware resulted. There is today, thus, no NATO antiballistic missile defense system comparable to the multinational Airborne Early Warning and Control System (AWACS), just as there is no ground counterpart to AWACS, meaning that U.S. Joint Stars aircraft largely fulfill this function.

At the Washington Summit five years later and in an environment where some twenty nations deploy ballistic missiles of theater range and two dozen are believed to be developing WMD capabilities, at U.S. initiative it was decided to "ensure a more vigorous, structured debate" including counter-WMD (hardware). The result, however, was yet another bureaucratic layer in the form of a WMD "Center" simply to exchange information, initiatives such as protective gear in a contaminated environment, and international warning and detection exercises (INTEX) with partners to develop procedures for warning and monitoring radioactive and other hazards to the civilian populations. While important, this is a reactive minimalist agenda and not a strategy for deterrence or counter- proliferation.

There are many reasons for the lack of movement, despite NATO highlighting WMD as a major risk and despite the 1999 U.S. National Security Strategy describing WMD as "the greatest potential threat." Some allies are not convinced of an emerging threat and still assign faith to arms control solutions and diplomacy. Some are geographically closer to the proliferators in North Africa and the Middle East and do not want NATO associated with what those nations might perceive as offensive preparations and lead to urban terrorist retaliation. Some might not agree to make their airspace or ground radar stations available for strikes (e.g., Denmark may not permit the upgrading of existing and deployment of new—"X-Band"—radar installations at Thule, Greenland, for U.S. kinetic energy National Missile Defense [NMD] purposes with one political factor being that the Greenlanders were deceived for many years by Copenhagen that despite a nuclear-weapon-free-zone, in fact, U.S. nuclear Nike Hercules warheads were stored there until 1965). Some have different political and arms sales relations with alleged proliferators than Washington. And some fear that by pursuing counter-WMD they could be dragged as an alliance into out-of-area activities and, as with Desert Storm, would prefer to leave this to the United States. But if WMD are indeed a real risk to NATO populations, then *NATO may be failing in its collective defense commitment and crisis management ability*, such that once again the burden may fall largely on the United States and the alliance succumbing to woeful negligence if not sheer recklessness.

Another problèmatique concerns the outcome of the U.S.-Russian discussions initiated in 1999 on the possible amendment of the 1972 ABM (Anti-Ballistic Missle) Treaty to allow for NMD against limited attacks, with only Russia maintaining and modernizing an area nuclear-armed ABM system, *Galosh* around Moscow, whereas the United States dismantled its permitted site in Grand Forks, North Dakota. Russia and key allies France, Germany, and the United Kingdom have opposed amendments as having the potential to undermine the fact of life of "mutually assured destruction" as a deterrent to the use of nuclear weapons, even though the U.S. motive is to counter rogue states such as Iran, Iraq, and North Korea (who may, by 2015 if not sooner, have the ability to launch intercontinental-range missiles) and not pose a threat to the nuclear arsenals of major powers. Russia will, therefore, have allies in NATO on this issue. The U.S. decision of September 1, 2000 not to authorize deployment of a NMD originally envisaged for 2005 in light of test failures and concerns expressed by Allies and Russia is not the final chapter, even if it may have been, as Lord Robertson artfully put it "a prudent course of action that balances the many factors involved." Theater missile defense—which of course is more relevant for Europe against proliferators south of the continent—is the immediate Pentagon priority (Patriot upgrade, Navy Area Defense Standard Missile, Airborne Laser, cruise missiles, Theater High Altitude Air Defense, Aegis Leap Intercept), but only Germany, Italy, and the Netherlands have collaborated with the United States. Here the failure of burden sharing is simply glaring, although it may prove a good area for U.S.–Russia cooperation, as noted in the joint "Strategic Stability Cooperation Initiative" signed in New York on September 6, 2000.

The U.S. permanent representative to the North Atlantic Council (NAC), Ambassador Alexander Vershbow, cautioned after the Washington Summit that "Allies may need to look more seriously at the possibility of theater missile defense," for proliferation is as much or even more a threat to Europe as it is to North America because of the higher likelihood of a closer-in-time theater-range threat.[32] However, in December 1999, more than half a year after WMDI was agreed at the Washington Summit, Secretary of Defense Cohen conceded "There is by no means a consensus within the Alliance."[33] Thus, all that was stated at the December 2, 1999 meeting of NATO defense ministers was "We are determined to improve our capabilities to address effectively the risks associated with the proliferation of weapons of mass destruction and their delivery means," but the communiqué spoke only about mere information sharing. The challenge for Washington will be to encourage the view at least among more like-minded allies that there is nothing necessarily incompatible with limited theater and longer range missile defenses, arms control, and strategic stability. With Russia and other NIS states, the United States pursues several programs for threat reduction such as the Stockpile Stewardship and Materials Protection Programs; the Trilateral Initiative among the United States, Russia, and the International Atomic Energy Agency (IAEA) to monitor excess military materials; and the Nuclear Cities (retraining nuclear workers), Proliferation Prevention (acquiring WMD expertise), and Long-Term Nonproliferation (managing fissile materials) initiatives.

In addition, although NATO has made a virtue of reducing its shorter range nuclear weapons based in Europe by 80 percent unilaterally and without reciprocity or transparency from Russia, which is believed to possess upwards of 10,000 nonstrategic nuclear warheads (about which Russia has been said to have not been forthcoming in discussions with NATO), it should review the role of nuclear deterrence in light of WMD challenges, including because NATO nations have disavowed biological and chemical weapons. Mutual Assured Destruction (MAD), as opposed to war fighting, may still make strategic sense in U.S.-Russian relations, and the U.S. NMD program is described as not threatening the Russian arsenal. But what is the strategy towards rogue states or even nonstate actors that may use or threaten to use WMD against NATO forces or territory? Has one iota of thought been given to the relationship between declining U.S. and Russian strategic nuclear arsenals and the limited NMD and its possible "breakout" potential to a full-scale NMD? Deterrence must be seen through a new lens, even though any use of nuclear weapons must remain one of last but not improbable resort: "it is difficult to attribute logic to the few [hundred] and aging [NATO-assigned] nuclear bombs deployed in Europe."[34] *Doing nothing could lower the nuclear threshold.*

COMMAND RESTRUCTURING

A major alliance task undertaken since fall 1994 has been the effort to achieve internal adaptation, with guidance initially given at the Brussels Summit earlier that year. A key vehicle in this difficult endeavor has been the work done by the Long-Term Study (L-TS). Its first task was to review and revise MC 400, a directive to NATO military commanders containing inter alia basic principles which the future command and force structure would have to satisfy.[35] The second aspect of the L-TS was the long and laborious effort to "reform" the integrated command structure, which was finally implemented on September 1, 1999.

Although this involved Herculean efforts to obtain agreement to support such a far-reaching reorganization, *the new command structure actually contains many fundamental weaknesses.*

As a general observation, NATO's effort was gravely hampered by political pressures emphasizing the need to "demonstrate" the new NATO and military concerns from the Major NATO Commanders (MNCs) who argued that reformed structures be based on military requirements—recommendations not necessarily in agreement.[36] This is, of course, an old tension in the alliance,[37] and the results of these almost immutable tensions can be seen in the following four areas of alleged reform to MC 324, "The NATO Military Command Structure":[38]

1. The levels of command will have new names to "demonstrate," perhaps, the alliance's transformation.

2. The number of headquarters (HQs) will shrink from sixty-five to twenty. But this "achievement" is less significant than meets the eye. Although the new structure abolishes the fourth command level, that of Subprincipal Subordinate Commands, many of these HQs are essentially national, such that very few of them will actually close.

3. Just as the number of MNCs fell from three to two in 1994 (eliminating the Channel Command prized by the United Kingdom), so too in Allied Command Europe (ACE) the number of Major Subordinate Commands (MSCs) at the second level will be reduced from three to two, i.e., eliminating Northwest in favor of North and South. This new NATO command rationalization was adopted despite SACEUR's recommendations for three regional commands to better execute the "span of command."[39] This is a familiar feature in the horse trading over national defense budgets, but all the same potentially crippling.

4. Subregional Commands will replace Principal Subordinate Commands (PSCs) and will either be specified as Component (single service) or Joint. Regional Commander South will see the creation of two new Joint Subregional Commands (JSRCs): "SouthWest" in Madrid and "SouthCenter" in Larissa, Greece. Two existing land Component Commands—Allied Land Force Southern Europe in Italy and Allied Land Forces Southeastern Europe in Turkey—will become JSRC "South" and "Southeast," respectively. Separate air and naval Component Commands will continue to exist. Missing from this reorganization, however, are land Component Commands which should act as the critical nexus between allied joint theater commanders on the one hand and multinational corps and national land armies on the other.

The above, in sum, represents the principal challenges which NATO thus far has been able to find consensus to support. At first blush, one might be forgiven in concluding that the new structure constitutes "old wine in a

Table 1-2
Previous NATO ACE Military Structure

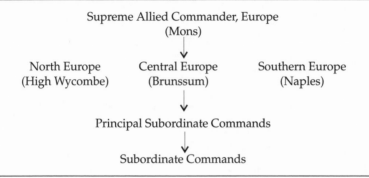

Supreme Allied Commander, Europe
(Mons)

North Europe   Central Europe   Southern Europe
(High Wycombe)   (Brunssum)   (Naples)

Principal Subordinate Commands

Subordinate Commands

Table 1-3
New NATO ACE Military Structure

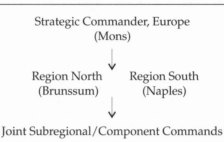

Strategic Commander, Europe
(Mons)

↓

Region North   Region South
(Brunssum)   (Naples)

↓

Joint Subregional/Component Commands

new bottle." Indeed, respected German defense correspondent Karl Feldmeyer argues that the L-TS results are but a redistribution of political influence among key allies, vice achieving greater military efficiency.[40] Yet, his views may arguably be an understatement. The structure endorsed at the Washington Summit actually contains a number of *potentially destructive trends* that, while perhaps politically palatable, could have long-term negative implications for the command of NATO military operations. One of the most detailed and persuasive assessments[41] of the L-TS command restructuring argues that the new structure:

- does *not* support Ministerial Guidance objectives established in MC 400/1 (the ability to undertake collective defense, PSOs, expansion of stability, and counterproliferation) and "seriously undermines the ability of the Alliance to meet its Article 5 obligations" by placing excessive pressure on fewer HQs, which may only be exacerbated by enlargement and the need to demonstrate the momentum of Partnership for Peace (PFP), even though that does not concern NATO's core function;
- will *only* be capable of conducting operations at the lower end of the threat spectrum; and
- through creating a national focus at the third level of command, the new structure will *inhibit* allied forces acting cohesively as a single entity and may encourage renationalization of defense. Indeed, NATO Military Committee Chairman General Naumann himself commented that the organization of NATO HQs has to be reviewed to make it more responsive to crisis response.[42]

Moreover, given that Supreme Headquarters Allied Powers Europe SHAPE and ACE underwent a 25 percent reduction in manpower, is the new staff composition sufficient to support the new structure?

FORCE STRUCTURE REVIEW

The third and final aspect of the L-TS is the Force Structure Review. It aims to review force structure requirements to support the new command structure and Ministerial Guidance for defense planning. The review will begin following agreed guidance on the military implications of the new Strategic Concept, together with an updating of NATO's operational planning procedures to take into account recent operations.

There is a degree of immediacy for the Force Structure Review, since it is becoming increasingly obvious that the multinational land force structures created since 1991 are not well suited to meeting allied strategy (Multinational Corps Northeast, 1 German/Netherlands Corps, V U.S./German Corps, II German/U.S. Corps, ACE Rapid Reaction Corps, Multinational Division Central, 1st United Kingdom Armored Division, 3rd United Kingdom Division, 3rd Italian Division, European Corps (EUROCORPS) and European Rapid Operational Force (EUROFOR). According to General Naumann:

Kosovo taught also and again that NATO's force structure, in contrast to NATO's Integrated Command Structure [although, as noted, he has suggested a review of the new organization], is no longer flexible and responsive enough to react quickly and decisively to unforeseen events. That we saw when Milosevic accelerated his expulsion of the Kosovars in an obvious attempt to counter NATO in an asymmetric response [Belgrade waged *war*, NATO conducted a limited, politically constrained "operation"] and to deprive NATO of its theoretical launching pad for ground forces operations through a destabilization of FRYOM and Albania. Luckily, we still had the Extraction Force [XFOR] in FYROM [a NATO force poised to pull out unarmed OSCE Kosovo Verification Mission (KVM) members; the KVM was withdrawn in early March 1999] and were thus able to react immediately. Without it, it would have taken NATO weeks to deploy and assemble an appropriate force [even though Yugoslavia adjoins new NATO member Hungary and lies just across the Adriatic from Italy]. The lesson learnt is that we have increasingly to be prepared for asymmetric responses . . . *it is critical for NATO's future successes to enhance mobility, flexibility and deployability of its forces, which are inadequate at this time.*[43]

In accord is his successor, Admiral Venturoni:

The actions to plan for are likely to be on a smaller scale than the scenarios envisaged during the Cold War. But they may last longer, in some cases require greater cooperation at lower levels of responsibility, and take place concurrently with other operations. This change in the way the Alliance expects to work makes crucial new demands on military forces and, specifically, the force structures that sustain them.

The requirement to react with joint forces simultaneously in a variety of theatres has already been partly addressed with the advent of the new Command Structure, which provides for regional commands and flexible joint operations. However, *the need to satisfy force levels and bring forces structures into line, so that we are able to react efficiently and effectively, remains the highest priority for the Military Committee.*[44]

As regards land forces and HQs declared to the alliance, three major problems predominate. First, most existing multinational land HQs and forces were created in the early 1990s with a view toward carrying out Article 5 missions and, in their present configuration, are unsuited to undertake non-Article 5 missions such as PSOs.

Second, operating practices under which these HQs are currently "commanded" do not allow commanders to exercise the command authority required to *prepare* their forces for their stated missions in peacetime, let alone deploy them effectively in crisis and war.

Third, there are currently an insufficient number of reaction HQs and similar forces capable of supporting the force structure benchmarks established by Ministerial Guidance for force planning.

For the L-TS to solve these problems, strict parameters need to be established to ensure that the review produces the results required to realign multinational HQs and forces declared to the alliance. In this respect, addressing the problems uniquely associated with multinational *land* HQs and declared forces need to predominate.

Land forces are the most difficult to command in a multinational setting given the requirement of multinational land force commanders to exercise greater authority over them than is required by naval and air multinational forces. Therefore, the alliance needs, for the first time, to establish new parameters under which multinational land HQs and forces are organized, commanded, and operated. It is not sufficient to review only "forces and headquarters." For without an examination of current command practices (for want of a better word), little in the way of real reform can result. In consequence, a number of important questions need to be addressed:

- What should be the basis of mission requirements of multinational land forces declared to the alliance?

- Do current multinational formations result in mismatches between requirements and capabilities?

- Where should existing multinational HQs' roles and missions be changed to improve the alliance's overall capabilities to meet Ministerial Guidance?

Mission Requirements of Multinational Land Forces

NATO does not suffer from a lack of multinational land HQs and formations declared to the alliance. There are currently six multinational corps (which includes the ambiguously declared EUROCORPS) and four multinational divisions declared to NATO. Added to this body is an ever-growing number of HQs established by nations and PFP states (e.g., Multinational Peace Force Southeastern Europe Brigade). However, the latter are predominantly oriented to undertake PSOs, as opposed to Article 5 missions. Significantly, they are not declared to the alliance and subject to the integrated defense planning process. Therefore, they fall outside of the terms of reference of the Force Structure Review.

Alliance strategy strongly endorses the concept of multinationality. That said, the effective use of multinational land forces is fiendishly difficult to achieve, as political sensitivities, national laws, and financial regulations impede granting an allied commander the command authorities normally given to a national commander.

Given the steep diminution in the size of NATO armies since the end of the cold war, the alliance is now heavily dependent upon the existence and effective functioning of HQs should it ever deploy forces. The alliance should insist, at a minimum, that multinational land HQs and subordinated forces are made capable of undertaking the core Article 5 mission. One recognizes that PSOs have taken on an increasingly important role in alliance defense planning, and this venue offers a unique opportunity to engage our partners in areas of mutual benefit.[45] Nonetheless, HQs and forces declared to the alliance do not exist solely for the purpose of engaging in PSOs, either exclusive of NATO's Partners or with them.

The Force Structure Review, therefore, should establish the baseline requirement that all multinational land formations declared to the alliance must be capable of conducting collective defense missions. Any move away from this standard might encourage nations to refocus their attention and orientation away from the basis of NATO. Moreover, an HQ and subordinated forces capable of conducting collective defense operations should also be capable of carrying out PSOs. Thus, the association of partner multinational HQs linked to existing NATO-declared HQs, while desirable and worthwhile from the long-term NATO perspective, should not be allowed to interfere with their primary mission of preparing to conduct collective defense operations. Partners should be encouraged to contribute, but they should be seen as complementing, vice supplementing, forces declared for collective defense.[46]

What Is the Lowest Appropriate Level for Multinational Land Formations?

National land forces declared to the alliance range from national corps (e.g., IV German Corps, Potsdam) to companies that contribute to the Immediate Reaction Force (Land). Since one of the principal objectives of the alliance's *raison d'être* is that nations declare forces to members' collective defense, allied commanders are ill-positioned to refuse national declarations of forces, irrespective of size. That said, sound military judgment must be proffered that explains to nations and alliance officials the simple fact that there are disadvantages to having formations made up of too many small contributions. The simple reason for this is that nations have yet to come to terms with the fact that multinational land formations are, by their very nature, less efficient and less effective than a similar purely national formation. Differences in language, weapons systems, organization, logistics, and procedures all hinder the effective operation of multinational formations. Compounding this truism is the added problem that the procedures by which national armies are declared to multinational HQs have not changed appreciably since the cold war, when nations' contributions in the Central Region were made at the national corps level; i.e., self-contained organizations.

Thus, the nettlesome issues of command authority requirements of a multinational force commander, transfer of command authority from a national to an allied commander, establishing logistics and training standards and priorities, etc., have yet to be revisited in depth since the widspread introduction of multinational structures in the Central Region. As a result, the alliance finds itself in the situation where it has transformed its diminished land forces in the Central Region into multinational formations that are largely unwieldy and difficult to prepare for war in peacetime and command in war. [47]

Notwithstanding these limitations, the alliance is hardly in the position to refuse forces declared by nations for collective defense. Nonetheless, NATO should establish more strict guidelines and measures that ensure declared forces are capable of contributing to the alliance's common objectives. In this respect, the suitable depth of multinational formations should be determined by a series of influencing factors, as opposed to arbitrary standards which nations are likely to oppose. The factors that determine the smallest size of a land force contribution to a multinational land formation are: (1) the size of a declared unit; and (2) the command authorities granted by nations to the multinational force commander.

Apropos the question of establishing a threshold for the minimum effective size of a force, the minimum size of suitable forces declared to the alliance should be, in large part, a function of their intended mission and related readiness levels. Thus, the political value of a national contribution to an Immediate Reaction Force (three to seven days readiness), no matter how "small," should be an overriding concern, whilst mobilization forces can be expected to be contributed in larger formations. A proposed generic minimum standard might be:

- Immediate Reaction Forces: select platoons, company, and battalion
- Rapid Reaction Forces: independent brigades with organic logistics
- Main Defense Forces: divisions with corps combat support and combat service support (CSS)
- Augmentation Forces: divisions and corps

Command Authorities

The delegation of command authorities (see Table 1-4) to multinational land force commanders remains one of the least developed areas of alliance force employment policy (see Table 1–5). Nations have been loath to give up command authorities over land forces to foreign commanders out of fear that, inter alia, they will be "fragmented" or improperly commanded. Yet, multinational land commanders require greater authority than they currently have over forces due to the complex nature of land forces, as opposed to aerial and naval units. More specifically, the missions and inherent operational limitations of aircraft and ships are a function of their very design. Land forces, on the other hand, are combined-arms teams that need to be organized to execute a mission. Thus, cross-assignment of forces (i.e., task-organization), the need oftentimes to change missions rapidly to respond to a developing situation, and the legitimate need for a commander to establish logistics priorities are some of the more sensitive issues nations are reluctant to give up to an allied commander.[48]

The proper place to analyze which command authorities a multinational force commander requires (employing the methodology of the 1994–1995 CR-CAST Working Group on the "Command Authorities Required by a Multinational Commander"—the only methodology developed to-date in this area), is with the assigned mission and an examination of the mission-essential tasks (stated and implied) therein.[49] Employing the CR-CAST methodology results in minimum requirements for a multinational corps commander (see Table 1-6).

Table 1-4
Definition of NATO Command Authorities

Operational Command (OPCOM). The authority granted to a commander to assign missions or tasks to subordinate commanders, to deploy units, to reassign forces, and to retain or delegate operational and/or tactical control as may be deemed necessary. It does not of itself include responsibility for administration or logistics. May also be used to denote the forces assigned to a commander.

Operational Control (OPCON). The authority delegated to a commander to direct forces assigned so that the commander may accomplish specific missions or tasks which are usually limited by function, time, or location, to deploy united concerned, and to retain or assign tactical control to those units. It does not include authority to assign separate employment of components of the units concerned. Neither does it, of itself, include administrative or logistic control.

Tactical Command (TACOM). The authority delegated to a commander to assign tasks to forces under his command for the accomplishment of the mission assigned by higher authority.

Tactical Control (TACON). The detailed and, usually, local direction and control of movements or maneuvers necessary to accomplish assigned missions or tasks.

Coordinating Authority (not a command authority). The authority granted to a commander of individual assigned responsibility for coordinating specific functions or activities involving forces of two or more countries or commands, or two or more services or two or more forces of the same service. He has the authority to require consultation between the agencies involved or their representatives, but does not have the authority to compel agreement. In case of disagreement between the involved agencies, he should attempt to obtain essential agreement by discussion. In the event he is unable to obtain agreement he shall refer the matter to the appropriate authority.

Source: MC 57/3, *Overall Organisation of the Integrated NATO Forces*, and AAP-6(U), *NATO Glossary of Terms and Definitions*, January 1995.

Table 1-5
Command Authorities of NATO and European Bi-/Multi-national Formations

1. Corps LANDJUT/"Multinational Corps Northeast"	OPCON/OPCOM* (in wartime) OPCON (in peacetime)[#]
2. I German/Netherlands Corps[+]	OPCOM (when employed)
3. V U.S./German Corps	OPCON (in wartime)
4. II German/U.S. Corps	OPCON (in wartime)
5. ACE Rapid Reaction Corps a. National Divisions b. Multinational Division (Central)[+]	OPCON (in wartime) OPCON>^

Bi-/multinational divisions declared to the ARRC:

6. 1st United Kingdom Armoured Division a. Danish International Mechanized Brigade b. 4th Czech *Brigáda rychlého Nasazení* (4th Rapid Reaction Brigade)	OPCON (in wartime) Coordinating Authority (in peacetime) OPCON $^\Sigma$
7. 3rd United Kingdom Division Italian *Ariete* Mechanized Brigade	OPCON (in wartime) Coordinating Authority (in peacetime)
8. 3rd Italian Division Portuguese Independent Airborne Brigade	OPCON (in wartime) Coordinating Authority (in peacetime
9. 7th German Panzer Division 10th Polish *Brygade Kawalerii Pancernej* (10th Armoured Cavalry Brigade)	OPCON $^\Sigma$
10. 1st U.S. Armoured Division 25th Hungarian *Klapka György Gépesített Lövész dandá* (25th Mechanized Infantry Brigade)	OPCON $^\Sigma$

European formations:

11. European Corps (EUROCORPS)[+]	OPCOM (when deployed)
12. European Rapid Operation Force (EUROPFOR)[+]	OPCON (when deployed)

*By agrement, Commander Corps LANDJUT has OPCON of forces under his command. However, in exercises, it has been the tradition for 30 years for Commander Corps LANDJUT to exercise OPCOM.

[+]"Force Answerable to the Western European Union (FAWEU)."

[#]The Corps Commander also now has "Integrated Directing and Control Authority." This authority provides the Commander with powers that are identical or similar to those vested in a commander of a national corps or with powers that are altogether new. Note

Table 1-5 continued

that sovereign rights (in the narrowest sense) are excepted. That said, the Corps Commander has the right to give instructions to all subordinate military and civilian personnel and may issue directives to the binational and national elements of the Corps and set priorities.

>Multinational Division (Central) headquarters is OPCOM to Commander ARRC in peacetime.

^Assigned brigades are under OPCON to Commander ARRC in peacetime.

ΣThe command authorities for these formations have yet to be fully confirmed via the NATO force generation process.

Table 1-6
Command Authority Recommendations

Article 5 collective defense: Operational Command (OPCOM)
Peace enforcement: OPCOM
Conflict prevention, peacemaking, peace building, humanitarian assistance: Operational Control (OPCON)

The rationale for the requirement of a higher command authority (OPCOM)—no NATO commander has "full command" over forces assigned to him because nations only assign OPCOM or OPCON for Article 5 and peace enforcement—is due to the need to carry out combat operations and for the commander to be capable of protecting the force. One should note that under current NATO procedures, OPCOM cannot be delegated by a strategic commander (he can only delegate OPCON) without prior political approval by the contributing nation.

In sum, given that multinational land forces declared to the alliance must be capable of conducting Article 5 missions, it is clear that the norm governing the delegation of command authority to a multinational commander should be OPCOM (without caveats), vice OPCON, with provision for revisions to the definition to include new authorities over peacetime training priorities and standards.

Multinational Practices Requiring Review

Current NATO procedures and the conditions under which nations declare forces and HQs to the alliance have not changed substantively since the end of the cold war, where multinational land formations were the rare exception. As a result, a number of debilitating practices and conditions combine to make successful peacetime planning challenging, and wartime operation problematic.

Logistics

An obvious weakness is the lack of sufficient CSS capabilities declared to formations. With the sole exception of the ACE Rapid Reaction Corps (ARRC) and Multinational Division (Central), no other multinational land

HQs has specific corps/division CSS capabilities declared to it. Given that logistics remain a national responsibility (notwithstanding the efforts of Central Region-Chiefs of Army Staff [CR-CAST] and Commander Allied Land Forces Central Europe [LANDCENT] to introduce concepts of multinationality to logistics), the practice of not declaring specific corps/division CSS formations limits effective peacetime planning and, potentially, wartime operation. Nations have had good reason not to declare specific CSS formations in that they are often cross-assigned to other multinational formations, or are treated as rare national treasures to be parceled out grudgingly only when absolutely required. The alliance needs to consider establishing minimum CSS standards by which nations declare forces to multinational formations. As the conflict in the former Yugoslavia demonstrates, combat forces without organic logistics and CSS are of limited operational utility to the alliance.[50]

Command Authorities

Concerning the issue of command authorities, the minimum requirements required were addressed earlier; however, the Force Structure Review should examine their definitions. The four recognized command authorities—OPCOM, OPCON, Tactical Command, and Tactical Control—have not been revised since the end of the cold war.[51] For example, two important issues for the success of a multinational force are not covered by current definitions. First, peacetime training remains a national, vice alliance, responsibility. A compromise solution would be for the alliance to establish an agreed set of tasks, conditions, and standards. The Military Committee, therefore, should direct the development of a robust "mission-essential task list" for land forces which could be used by multinational force commanders to validate established training standards.[52] While perhaps only applicable to the 1 German/Netherlands Corps where deep integration has been established as an essential political objective, the development by those two nations of "Integrated Directing and Control Authority" may provide a useful example of what can be accomplished in this area. This unique command authority provides the corps commanding general with powers that are identical or similar to those vested in a commander of a national corps or with powers that are altogether new. Of course, sovereign rights (in the narrowest sense) are excepted from the commander's purview. That said, the corps commander has the right to give instructions to all subordinate military and civilian personnel and may issue directives to the binational and national elements of the corps and set priorities.

Second, closely related to the issue of command authorities and training is the question of when forces "transfer" ("transfer of authority"—TOA) from nations to a multinational land force commander. It is unrealistic to assume that nations will surrender the operational employment of their forces well before their deployment. Yet, greater clarity in doctrine is needed as to when forces should transfer to a multinational force commander, i.e., prior to, or immediately upon, arrival in the theater of operations. Frictions between multinational force commanders and nations can be expected until such time that important issues like training priorities and standards are addressed.

HQ Interoperability

There exists no standard organizational "template" by which the multinational land HQs declared to the alliance adhere. As demonstrated in the SFOR experience, three NATO division HQs were deployed to the theater under the ARRC. These divisions included subordinated forces with which these HQs had no peacetime habitual training relationships (to include units from non-NATO nations). HQs declared to the alliance, therefore, should be required to adhere to a number of basic standards, the better to enable them to integrate forces with which they do not have a peacetime planning and exercising relationship. Headquarters declared to NATO should have NATO international legal personality to facilitate their employment by the alliance, with all falling under the "Protocol on the Status of International Military Headquarters set up pursuant to the North Atlantic Treaty" concluded in Paris on August 28, 1952.

Headquarters declared to NATO should adopt as a minimum those procedures and practices established in formal Military Committee guidance, NATO Standardization Agreements (STANAGs), Allied Tactical Publication 35, and the planning guidelines emerging from Bi-Major NATO Command working groups supporting Combined Joint Task Force (CJTF) concept development. HQs declared to NATO must use English as their official language, with greater provision for the use of French when requested.

Changing Roles and Missions of Existing HQs and Forces

Multinational corps in the Central Region were established in the early 1990s with the view of providing nations the ability to operate competently within a corps structure, but with smaller force structures. With the obvious exception of the ARRC, all other multinational corps have an alliance main defense, not rapid reaction, mission. Notwithstanding the fact that some have the ability to engage in PSOs, the ARRC remains the alliance's sole reaction corps.

There are currently insufficient suitable HQs and forces capable of supporting the force structure benchmarks established by Ministerial Guidance for defense planning. For example, the alliance has created three CJTF-designed HQs (Regional Commander North, Regional Commander South, and Commander Striking Fleet Atlantic). Additionally, guidance from ministers and the Defense Review Committee hold that Strategic Command Europe must be prepared to undertake two non-Article 5 contingencies, as well as an Article 5 contingency. Yet, the alliance has available for rapid reaction missions only two land component commands to support a CJTF, i.e., ACE Rapid Reaction Corps and the Immediate Reaction Force-Land (the latter of which is only capable of commanding and controlling a large brigade). It is for this reason that the alliance was forced to accept the use of the EUROCORPS as a follow-on KFOR HQ in 2000 because of a lack of suitable reaction HQs declared to the alliance. Thus, *there is a need for additional multinational land HQs, declared to the alliance, with a reaction focus*, vice largely less relevant HQs and forces with solely main defense missions. The very lack of a ground component HQ for Kosovo was highlighted by Admiral James Ellis, Commander-in-Chief, Allied Forces Southern Europe; Commander-in-Chief U.S. Naval Forces, Europe; and Commander, Joint Task Force Noble Anvil (during Allied Force) as constituting a major mistake in the conduct of the campaign against the Federal Republic of Yugoslavia (FRY) in 1999.[53]

Six points should guide the designation and creation of new reaction corps HQs:

1. existing corps-size multinational main defense HQs could be redesignated;

2. there are sufficient reaction force divisions declared to the alliance generally to meet current Ministerial Guidance 1999 requirements;

3. reaction force divisions and corps CSS should be declared to newly designed reaction corps HQs to ensure the development of habitual working relationships;

4. efforts at creating effective multinational land formations heretofore have been almost exclusively limited to Region North armies. The Force Structure Review offers nations the opportunity to establish potentially similar structures that offer many nondefense advantages in Region South. Region North nations and armies, in particular, should participate more actively in a Region South reaction force HQ and declare reaction forces and corps CSS in order to bring their technological expertise to bear and to contribute to establish a conductive working and operating environment;

5. the designation of certain HQs as "light" and "heavy" oriented would result in limiting alliance deployment options as opposed to increasing them. Reaction force HQs, perforce, must be capable of operating within the full spectrum of missions and conditions; and

6. finally, and perhaps most importantly, any new reaction force HQs must adhere to the principles of multinationality outlined above in order to be capable of integrating subordinated forces and serve effectively as a CJTF's multinational land component command HQ.

The alliance should consider a multifaceted approach to meeting the requirement for an increased number of HQs capable of serving as land component HQs under a CJTF. Major political decisions need to be made by nations and financial resources committed to this objective if the alliance is to achieve this ambitious goal.

Options for Reform

The ARRC (Mönchengladbach) has a proven record as a multinational reaction force HQ (IFOR and KFOR) and is the only one with declared corps CSS. That it remains largely British-dominated (60 percent of the HQ is British) is a political weakness that can be overcome by an increase in other corps-sized reaction force HQs. That said, additional reaction force corps, perforce, should draw upon the current unwieldy eleven divisions declared to it since ARRC is only capable of commanding, on deployment, four divisions.

V US/II German Corps

The U.S. Army in Europe is the best prepared to conduct reaction force missions in Europe. However, its corps HQs, being national, would require the most internal reform. Currently, V U.S. Corps (Heidelberg) has a wartime arrangement to cross-assign divisions with II GE Corps (Ulm). The alliance would be very well served indeed if V U.S. and II GE Corps were merged, with the United States as the lead nation, and transformed into an alliance reaction force HQ with international personality. Divisions currently declared to the ARRC could be reassigned to the new corps.

I German/Netherlands Corps

This formation (Münster) was initially designed for main defense missions and, in effect, to merge the two armies. However, the Royal Netherlands Army is undergoing a significant restructuring and reorganization, better enabling it to engage in power-projection missions. The German Army has also made progress in creating crisis reaction forces. Both nations should strongly consider reorienting the HQ primarily toward a reaction force. The HQ's strong adherence to NATO standards and the use of English make it highly suitable. Divisions declared to the ARRC could be reassigned to give it greater force structure depth. To be sure, it would be unique in that it would not be a lead nation formation, but rather binational.

EUROCORPS

Because this formation (Strasbourg) includes the French Army, it offers considerable operational advantages to the alliance, especially given France's extensive experience in power projection. However, the French Army remains equally unfamiliar with basic NATO procedures. An example of its heretofore "distant" relationship with NATO is that only as of September 1, 1999, was English made the operational language of the HQ. Moreover, the corps is multiroled, is not combat ready for use as a reaction force, and enjoys, at best, an ambiguous relationship with the alliance. The nations participating in this formation could make a major contribution to the alliance if they were to: (1) clearly declare the HQ to the alliance; (2) reorganize the HQ to adhere to standards outlined above; and (3) adopt, unambiguously, a reaction force mission and orientation.[54]

Options in Region South

Probably the alliance's biggest challenge is to establish a reaction force HQ that fosters improved interoperability among Region South armies. Traditionally, the armies of this region have had limited opportunity to work together in a peacetime multinational setting, let alone on deployment. Two allies—Greece and Turkey—even concluded a nonaggression agreement between them in the 1990s. And, indeed, the decision by the alliance not to create land component commanders in Regions North and South (whereas there are air and sea component commanders) places obstacles in the path of improving this situation. As a result, there will not be a suitable land-focused HQ acting to integrate armies during peacetime, let alone providing a capability to the alliance to act as a land component commander under a CJTF.

Nonetheless, at the level of forces and HQs, the alliance can work to overcome this current lack of multinationality. The most obvious option relates to the European Rapid Operational Force (EUROFOR, with HQ in Florence), a division-size HQ currently not declared to the alliance. Participants include Italy, France, Spain, and Portugal. As is the case with EUROCORPS, the current status of EUROFOR contributes little to alliance planning and preparations, although it has the potential. Being in Italy, it is located in the central Mediterranean and enjoys modern and extensive infrastructure. Greece and Turkey should be encouraged to declare reaction forces to it. The HQ should be: (1) expanded eventually to the size of a corps staff; (2) declared to the alliance; (3) reorganized to adhere to standards for HQ outlined above; (4) North American and Region North staff officers should be assigned to the HQ; and (5) North American and Region North forces should be declared to it.

Rationalization of HQs?

The above analysis intentionally did not address the suitability of Multinational Corps Northeast (Szczecin) and IV German Corps (Potsdam). There is merit in maintaining a number of multinational corps with largely a main defense orientation. However, those formations that retain this mission orientation would contribute greatly to the alliance's main defense capabilities by inviting the armies of the new NATO members to declare forces to the formations and participate in the HQ staffs. Other alliance members should second staff officers also to these formations and contribution to their operation.

The Way Ahead

Nations face considerable challenges in reforming the structures and practices regulating the operation and command of multinational land

HQs. The Force Structure Review offers nations a unique opportunity to re-examine these problems and lacunae in stated alliance strategy and Ministerial Guidance on the one hand, and current structures and capabilities on the other. On the negative side of the task, nations have traditionally been reluctant to offer up land forces to foreign commanders, and national laws make a multinational land force commander's influence over such issues as logistics challenging at best. However, on the positive side, there is little need for nations to create new forces and HQs. Rather they need to reexamine the missions of currently existing HQs. That said, let there be no doubt that without a fresh review of the practices and authorities under which multinational land force commanders currently comand their forces, a mere redesignation of HQs' missions will be for naught. In late 2000, Chairman Venturoni, noting that NATO had not changed its force structure since the early 1990s, imagined possibly three land corps with comparable air and naval forces at high readiness, and possibly up to six land corps at lower readiness for sustained operations.[55]

COMBINED JOINT TASK FORCES

An issue that has baffled NATO officials and nations is the dreadfully slow development of a formal, endorsed concept for CJTF.[56] One of the key initiatives to be adopted at the 1994 Brussels Summit was endorsement of the European Security and Defense Identity (ESDI), since 1999, termed by the EU the Common European Security and Defense Policy (CESDP)—even though neither an "identity" or "policy" have come to life. CJTF was envisaged to be the means by which NATO could not only undertake its own Article 5 or non-Article 5 missions more flexibly, but support operations by the Western European Union (WEU), the ten-member security forum independent of both NATO and the EU. The 1991 NATO Strategic Concept had already required "enhanced flexibility and mobility and an assured capacity for augmentation when necessary."

CJTF is a relatively modest and simple concept. A CJTF HQ is a deployable, multinational, joint HQ of variable size involving no new structures, with the ability to deploy quickly to the area of operations. Its purpose is to command subordinated NATO and non-NATO forces from collective defense to OOTWs. Yet, notwithstanding this innocuous and seemingly commonsense initiative, the concept languished because of the difficulty in finding acceptance among nations of how NATO would support ESDI and ongoing disagreements. These are, predictably, between Washington and Paris over issues related to the integrated command structure, the European weight in it, and the chain-of-command for a WEU-led operation and the role of the NATO "supporting" commander. However, by the time of the May 1996 NATO Berlin Ministerials, the NATO-led CJTF-like IFOR had already been operating without the theory finalized. At the 1997 Madrid Summit, the Military Committee was directed to recommend implementation steps, emphasizing the need for pilot trials. This led to a three-phase implementation program:

- Phase 1 (1996–1998): Three parent HQs were designated CJTF HQs at the second level of the then command structure and an initial capability concept was developed. Two trials were held to ascertain HQ requirements such as size, manning, and structure.
- Phase 2 (1998–1999): The results of the trials were evaluated.
- Phase 3 (1999–?): Full implementation,[57] to include dealing with "a number of unanswered or only partially answered questions" including expenses, a timetable for full implementation, and meeting the political expectations of the CJTF Concept.[58]

Other factors at work beyond the precise command role NATO would exercise over a non-NATO CJTF are the contentious development of ESDI/CESDP and the overarching so-called EU Common Foreign and Security Policy (CFSP). The appointment in 1999 of NATO Secretary General Javier Solana to his new position as secretary general of the EU Council of Ministers and high representative for CFSP, and also as WEU secretary general, may expedite matters. But it is still unclear what new powers he will assume at the expense of EU national governments, let alone what his relationship will be relative to Chris Patten, EU commissioner for external affairs (for example, at the December 1999 NATO Brussels NAC Ministerial, Solana attended with his WEU, not EU, "hat"). Just as a formal NATO-WEU cooperation agreement was still not reached as 1999 ended, despite work since 1994, a NATO-EU cooperation agreement did not even achieve an interim status. In addition, a significant problem that remains to be resolved concerns the legal and political constraints nations may face in providing collective assets to a non-NATO operation. For example, it remains a question as to whether the U.S. Code would support as lawful the use of U.S. assets to support a non-NATO military campaign. And how willing will nations be to work with the counterpart to CJTF, the Multinational Joint Logistics Center (MJLC) announced at the Washington Summit (even though the concept has been tested in Bosnia and Kosovo), inasmuch as logistics has traditionally been a national responsibility?

Thus, although CJTF might very well represent an example of practice without theory, important unanswered political questions remain to be resolved if the alliance is not to be impeded in its planning and execution of this important command and control concept. As progress is measured, it must be recalled that, citing General Naumann: "the fact that CJTFs may play a role in the collective defense task of NATO was an important consideration, among others, that led NATO to decide to forego any stationing of NATO headquarters on the territories of the three countries invited to join"[59] (although "infrastructure" will be permitted because of the reliance on reinforcement).

2

THE EUROPEAN DIMENSION

The Atlantic nations must join in a fresh act of creation, equal to that undertaken by the postwar generation of leaders of Europe and America. . . . We need a shared view of the world we seek to build.[1]

Henry A. Kissinger
April 23, 1973

The construction of an integrated Europe will be incomplete as long as it does not include security and defense.

WEU Hague Platform
October 27, 1987

There is probably no other issue in NATO traditionally more subject to grossly inflated national egotism and posturing than the so-called European Security and Defense Identity (ESDI). Today, as in the past, there is the view that the alliance was always one "in which the United States makes unilateral decisions and expects loyalty" from the allies,[2] but the military problems of achieving greater European responsibility and capacity to act themselves contribute to a European willingness to let the United States lead. The crisis in Yugoslavia only reinforced this complacency.

However, there are signals, although they have emerged in the past only to come to naught, that political attention to the possibility of a "common European defense," as phrased in the 1991 Treaty of Maastricht, has increased. In addition to the European diplomatic dominated UN Protection

Force/(UNPROFOR) fiasco in Yugoslavia until NATO stepped in, this momentum is propelled by a sense that a common European currency must be matched by common security policies, and a more permissive view by the United States (and the United Kingdom) towards an independent European capability, albeit one also serving as the European "pillar" of the alliance. Additionally, "Increased discussion in Europe of ESDI is a manifestation of the Allies' recognition that significant elements of U.S. political leadership are hesitant about the use of American combat forces for [humanitarian intervention], and that Europeans must be prepared to act alone," even if "Most smaller NATO and EU members, concerned about domination by one of the larger [European] member states, greatly prefer U.S. leadership from afar to political elbowing from a neighbor."[3]

French President Jacques Chirac called attention to "the present situation [of one superpower] is causing difficulties in numerous countries, including the most powerful among them, the United States, where Congress too often gives in to the temptations of unilateralism and isolationism."[4] French Foreign Minister Hubert Védrine, a Socialist, questioned whether the United States would be willing to accept "more than a limited or momentary partnership" with Europe and graduate from unilateralism to multilateralism, issues which he stated underlay "the whole question of the European common foreign and defense policy,"[5] and he has contrasted U.S. calls for burden sharing with reluctance to share decision making. According to Commissioner Patten: "What we're trying to do is to make sure the European voice is heard at the same strong decibel level as when the European Union speaks as the world's biggest trade bloc and the biggest foreign aid donor."[6]

The reality was described by French Defense Minister Alain Richard: "I tell my American friends that one day I hope they will be able to have as much confidence in European defense capabilities as they have in the Australians in East Timor,"[7] whereas former Swedish Prime Minister Carl Bildt described CFSP as "little more than an academic exercise in Brussels."[8] The Europeans are habituated to creating lucrative tax-exempt positions and bloated bureaucracies, even if the substance is often overwhelmed by process and the illusion of progress. For example, During Desert Storm a senior French deputy was asked by one of the coauthors why France was not contributing more forces and responded: "*Come on*. It's an *American* show" (France, Italy, and the United Kindom contributed only 6 percent of the forces).

FROM BERLIN TO HELSINKI

Nevertheless, an apparent breakthrough in this long-standing discussion (since the failure of the multinational-force European Defense Community in 1954) was supposedly reached at the NATO Berlin Ministerials. There, the allies, as noted, endorsed the development of the European Security and Defense Identity "within the Alliance." This would include preparations through CJTFs for WEU-led operations and identification of "separable but not separate capabilities" and appropriate European command positions within NATO, such as "double-hatting" the deputy SACEUR for both NATO and WEU-led operations, or perhaps returning to a three-regional command structure with one commanded by a EU/WEU-dedicated focus (although this could prove an obstacle if a NATO and WEU operation occurred simultaneously).

Then, in the EU Treaty of Amsterdam of June 1997, the EU members, including four "non-aligned" nations of Austria, Ireland, Sweden, and Switzerland ("free-riders" to others), agreed to consider contributing to the WEU 1992 "Petersberg Tasks" (named after an area in Bonn) concerning missions other than collective defense: humanitarian and rescue operations, peacekeeping, and "tasks of combat forces in crisis management including peacemaking" (the last term meaning diplomatic actions including sanctions to bring warring parties to a peaceful settlement). This decision took the EU a step closer, as the Treaty of Amsterdam states, to "the progressive framing of a *common defense policy* . . . which might lead to a *common defense*, should the European Council so decide" (emphasis added). This WEU-EU interface was suggested in April 1996 by Swedish Foreign Minister Lena Hjelm-Wallen and Finnish Foreign Minister Tarja Halonen.[9] It and the subsequent Amsterdam Treaty fell far short, however, of German Chancellor Helmut Kohl's suggestion earlier that year that a "solidarity clause" akin to Article 5 of the NATO and WEU treaties be added to the EU *acquis*, arguing that "It cannot be the case that within the EU, which we understand to be a community based on solidarity, there are those who are responsible for security and defense on the one hand and those who are responsible for trade on the other hand."[10]

This rationale did not explain, nonetheless, why the same states belonging to WEU and NATO, NATO members, and the military neutral EU member/WEU observer states would coexist with three similar collective defense guarantees (a problem which the likely merger of WEU and EU has yet to address). Also, the United Kingdom opposed granting full decision-making rights for neutral EU members in WEU operations requested by the EU as this "would marginalize WEU Associate Members [non-EU NATO states] who share mutual defense obligations."[11]

Thereafter, a joint Franco-British declaration emerged in December 1998 in St. Malo, France, urging that the EU be able to take decisions and military action where NATO as a whole is not engaged, requiring European capabilities "pre-designated within NATO's European pillar or national or multinational European means outside the NATO framework." This was not quite the same as the Brussels Ministerial language concerning development of ESDI "within the Alliance," but presumably the leaders were taking into account the possibility that the United States, or any non-EU NATO member, could always block the release of NATO assets and CJTF HQs.

A few months later, this formula was adopted at the EU Cologne Council on June 3, 1999: "The Union must have the capacity for autonomous action, backed up by credible military forces, the means to decide to use them, and a readiness to do so, in order to respond to international crises without prejudice to actions by NATO." Further work was ordered on an EU Presidency Report which stated that the EU will have to determine whether it will conduct "EU-led operations using NATO assets and capabilities or EU-led operations without recourse to NATO and capabilities [using] national or multinational European means pre-identified by Member States." The EU will consider "facilitating the participation of Russia when the EU avails itself of the WEU for missions within the range of the Petersberg tasks" and will ensure that arrangements exist for non-EU NATO nations to participate. A military committee and a military staff would be considered. Further progress would be sought in "the harmonization of military requirements and the planning and procurement of arms as Member States consider appropriate." The EU would also "foster the restructuring of the European defense industries . . . towards closer and more efficient [read competitive with the United States] defense industry collaboration" (defense industries had traditionally been excluded from EU treaties). Eventually, the moribund WEU, which proved unable to act in Albania in 1997 reportedly because of British and German objections, would merge with the EU.

On November 23, 1999, the WEU issued an "Audit of Assets and Capabilities for European Crisis Management Operations" underlining the following "most urgent efforts": strategic intelligence and planning; availability; deployability; strategic mobility; sustainability; survivability; interoperability; operational effectiveness, combined joint operation and force HQs with particular reference to command, control, communications, and deployability. This was still nothing more than what the very same nations had agreed to in the DCI over half a year before, whereas as long ago as 1992 the WEU agreed on "the need to develop a genuine European security and defense identity and a greater European responsibility in defense matters."

U.S. Deputy Secretary of State Talbott then spoke of "apprehensions" which St. Malo and Cologne had generated with respect to the Berlin Ministerial decisions:

It's in our interest for Europe to be able to deal effectively with challenges to European security well before they reach the threshold of triggering U.S. combat involvement . . . [but] We would not want to see an ESDI that comes into being first within NATO but then grows out of NATO and finally grows away from NATO, since that would lead to an ESDI that initially duplicates NATO but that could eventually compete with NATO. That's a long-term concern, obviously, but NATO, after all, is about the long term.[12]

The Washington Summit communiqué reaffirmed "our commitment to preserve the transatlantic link, including our readiness to pursue common security objectives *through the Alliance wherever possible*" (emphasis added). But reflecting the uncertainty about the nuances of language used in NATO and EU statements, the Washington Summit communiqué could only record "The presumption of availability to the EU of pre-identified NATO capabilities and common assets for use in EU-led operation" with the "necessary arrangements" still being finalized. At the EU Summit in Helsinki on December 10, 1999, these carefully-phrased guidelines were agreed flowing from the Cologne directives:

The European Council underlines its determination to develop an autonomous capacity to take decisions and, where NATO as a whole is not engaged, to launch and conduct EU-led military operations in response to international crises. This process will avoid unnecessary duplication and does not imply the creation of a European army. . . .

The European Council has agreed in particular the following:

- cooperating voluntarily in EU-led operations, Member States must be able, by 2003, to deploy within 60 days and sustain for at least 1 year military forces of up to 50,000–60,000 [Eurocorps] persons capable of the full range of Petersberg tasks [the so-called "headline goal" (former NATO Military Committee Chairman General Naumann believes 14 days is a more relevant notice to move)];
- new political and military bodies and structures will be established within the Council to enable the Union to ensure the necessary political guidance and strategic direction to such operations, while respecting the single institutional framework [interim structures were established by March 2000];
- modalities will be developed for full consultation, cooperation and transparency between the EU and NATO, taking into account the needs of all EU Member States;
- appropriate arrangements will be defined that would allow, while respecting the Union's decision-making autonomy, non-EU European NATO members and other interested States to contribute to EU military crisis management;
- a non-military crisis management mechanism will be established to coordinate and make more effective the various civilian means and resources, in parallel with the military ones, at the disposal of the Union and the Member States.

With respect to the new structures, it was agreed to establish a standing Political and Security Committee, a military committee, and a military staff to undertake "early warning" (supposedly the role of the OSCE), situation assessment, and strategic planning for Petersberg tasks, including identification of European national and multinational forces (the exact same function the WEU "Planning Cell" had taken in 1993 only to fire no shots in anger ever). No effort was made to suggest a NATO-EU division of labor or clarify how ESDI/CESDP would evolve "within the Alliance." For example, might EU NATO allies focus excessively on non-Article 5 planning, how and would the nonaligned EU states relate to the NATO integrated military structure and NATO's collective defense tasks, and would the EU with its separate structures make it more difficult for NATO to take decisions? The Presidency Report to the Helsinki Summit noted that "NATO remains the foundation of the collective defense of its members, and will continue to have an important role in crisis management." Yet, Lord Robertson stated on December 15, 1999: "Intentions are very good and new institutions are very useful. But it is results that count. ESDI will be judged first and foremost by the capabilities that it delivers to the EU and to the Alliance" (only Greece and Turkey meet the U.S. Congressional target of approximating the U.S. defense budget as a share of GDP, but all are subject to pressures on the defense budget). Robertson insists upon what he terms the "three I's":

- improvements in European defense capabilities
- inclusiveness of the non-EU NATO allies in common efforts (Canada, Iceland, Norway, Turkey, and the United States)
- indivisibility of the transatlantic link[13]

The Clinton administration refers to the "three D's" no decoupling, no duplication, no discrimination.

In reaction, U.S. NATO Ambassador Vershbow commented, perhaps reflecting a continuously-denied preference for an unchallenged NATO (US) *über Alles* approach:

[I]t's not the end of the debate, and there are some issues that still have to be worked on in the coming weeks and months . . . we did have some problems with the way these issues were treated in Cologne—not in the larger sense, but because there were some details that we felt were not treated quite as we had hoped. For example, in Washington there was a very clear statement that, as Allies, we will try to act through NATO 'wherever possible.' This reflected the fact that if we are dealing with crisis management or peace enforcement it is certainly always better if we can act with the broadest possible coalition and with the broadest possible military capability to back up our political strategy. The Cologne decision seemed to suggest a desire on the part of the European Union to become the 'option of first resort,' rather than an alternative to NATO. . . . But over the past few months, we have been working very intensively and very closely together. I think that, from the Washington perspective, the results of Helsinki were very positive . . . They certainly seem to have pointed the European enterprise in a direction that is a little more 'NATO-friendly.' Most importantly, the Helsinki decisions were very explicit and very ambitious on the issue of capabilities.[14]

He went on to stress U.S. concerns that non-EU NATO European states be involved in EU-led actions, and that the NATO-EU institutional relationship move beyond the occasional and informal Robertson-Solana breakfasts on a provisional or interim basis until the EU makes its own decisions about the internal structures to support the CESDP, which he stated should not be postponed until the EU put the final touches on all of its internal structures.

Ambassador Vershbow subsequently elaborated:

It is true that we have had some spirited discussions of ESDI in NATO this year. It is also true that we are not in agreement on every detail of its development with our EU Allies.

We have essentially based our support for ESDI in the EU context on four points. These were all agreed in Washington, although things got a bit muddled when the EU met two months later in Cologne. Since then, the EU has moved to deliver on two. These are the four issues for us:

- NATO first. We should not have to haggle in a crisis situation over whether NATO is the instrument of choice . . . if the U.S. is prepared to participate, wouldn't it be foolish—if not risky—to turn us down?

- Capabilities. . . . We need to avoid separate EU and NATO planning systems that lead to different standards for EU and other Allies' forces. That could lead to a two-tier Alliance, weakening our ability to work together in a major crisis.

- Participation. Six European NATO Allies are not EU members . . . and that number may grow if NATO enlargement continues to outpace EU enlargement. . . . The EU has expressed a commitment to include the six in some fashion, but this is unfinished business for now.

- NATO-EU links . . . The EU is curiously reluctant to move forward on establishing such links. . . . This is also unfinished business.[15]

A FRESH ACT OF CREATION

Despite these lingering questions, obviously if the DCI is implemented then European confidence could be bolstered, even if that would not automatically translate into the political will to act when the United States chooses not to do so. The very same European forces will operate under NATO or another command, and it would be duplicative and, in view of the EU membership of four "non-aligned" nations and the absence of a supporting CFSP, not credible for the EU to duplicate NATO's collective defense and crisis management structures. But the imbedded suspicions on both sides of the Atlantic cannot block progress indefinitely if there is to be a strong European pillar of NATO and a credible, autonomous ESDI/CESDP.

Even if institutional issues and capabilities remain at issue, even though an EU-led Petersberg operation can evolve into a NATO mission, and whether or not Minister Védrine's comment suggests that ESDI is perhaps too closely linked to U.S. behavior rather than a worthy product of the logic of European integration, the goal must firmly remain achieving a better equilibrium between the two sides of the Atlantic. It is nonsensical that the WEU ministers, meeting in Luxembourg on November 23, 1999, could only welcome the "intention" of the EUROCORPS to adapt "to the new strategic environment"—and then not even until 2003! Why should more be expected of the EU than the WEU? Indeed, would Europe's paralysis in Bosnia prior to the Dayton General Framework Agreement of November 1994 be reinforced within NATO because of a prior EU position, just as it was the Europeans who were reluctant to continue the bombing campaign that made Dayton possible? Why will the EU prove more willing to increase resources when they have not done so as NATO allies, despite the argument of François Heisbourg noted in chapter 1 that the EU could provide political impetus?

Getting the ESDI-NATO balance right will invariably prove a perpetual process of managing contradictions:

- between rhetoric and hardware;
- between European declaration to take on greater responsibility, but a reluctance to act without the United States and U.S. leadership (witness the Balkans);
- between a vocation towards a common defense policy and the absence of a coherent CFSP;
- between European aspirations to be a global security actor, but a European reluctance to cede leadership to any one or group of European states, cf. unchallenged U.S. leadership of NATO;
- between those European aspirations to act in solidarity, but a lacuna regarding shared European nuclear deterrence;
- between a declared European agreement to develop ESDI within NATO, but reluctance to establish early and transparent EU-NATO working relations, including coordination of defense planning; and
- between U.S. calls for greater European responsibility, but refusal to countenance any "EU caucus" within NATO or the lack of a voice even when the United States does not participate in EU-led missions, should they ever occur on a meaningful military scale, and willingness only to allow the "presumption" of the availability of NATO assets as decided by NATO (with a U.S. veto) to European operations.

Nevertheless, it is to be welcomed that both NATO and WEU held a crisis management exercise, CMX-CRISEX 2000, in February 2000 to manage simultaneously a NATO Article 5 and a WEU peacekeeping operation with NATO providing assets to WEU. This was the first time that procedures built up over the better part of the 1990s were tested. Moreover, as Lord

Robertson has observed: "In the last 18 months Europe has made more progress on ESDI than in 18 years before," although "capabilities remain the ultimate litmus test for ESDI."[16] On September 19, 2000 the first meeting was held between the NAC and the EU interm Political and Security Committee, with working groups continuing discussions on political and operational arrangements between the two organizations (it was predicted that WEU would expire within the coming months).

As always, *the problem is not too much America in Europe, but too little Europe*. As this fitful process proceeds, Congress must insist that the administration, and ideally NATO as a whole, although that seems improbable because of a tradition of nontransparency, provide regular meaningful and not predetermined "good news" progress reports (aka "mushroom treatment" that tailor important information) on how all allies are or are not meeting DCI goals. It seems at best a whitewash, for instance, that the combat shortfalls during Allied Force prompt hope for DCI, but that earlier in 1999 the Pentagon concluded "[NATO] country efforts present a mixed but generally positive picture in terms of shouldering responsibility for shared security objectives"[17]—perhaps out of concern that Congress could try to force the burden-sharing issue. But should measurable progress be made, then the United States should be prepared to reassess the national proportion of the key NATO commands, with at present the two second layers of allied command vested with the United States. But the burden of proof is on Europe.

3

WHAT PRICE HONOR?

The sovereignty of states can constitute an essential bulwark against intimidation or coercion, but it must not be allowed to obstruct effective action to address problems that transcend borders or to secure human dignity.[1]

Kofi A. Annan
1998

We remain determined to stand firm against those who violate human rights, wage war, and conquer territory.

The NATO Washington Declaration
April 23, 1999

Today, it is widely recognized that the concept of "humanitarian intervention" can be legitimate as a last resort. "Classic" international law must never serve as an alibi for rulers whose objective is ethnic cleansing and human suffering.

Niels Helveg Petersen
Minister of Foreign Affairs, Denmark
June 29, 2000

10 years for Human Rights in Foreign Policy

Pernille Bonnesen
Royal Danish Embassy, Washington D.C.
June 29, 2000

The first thing we do, let's kill all the lawyers.

William Shakespeare
Henry VI, Part 2 IV: 2

Even were the full spectrum of alliance capabilities in place, the ultimate question involves the "political will" and international legal authority to act to secure stability with sustainable justice despite a fluid status quo. As noted, the Washington Treaty provides two routes for the use of force:

- Article 5 collective defense against attack, and
- Article 4 (also termed "non-Article 5") cooperation in crisis management and to address any ally's security concerns.

The Treaty does not affect the primary responsibility of the UNSC for the maintenance of international peace and security and to determine threats to it and measures to restore it, but the Charter recognizes the preexisting inherent right of collective- and self-defense. It further allows for the use of force consistent with the "Purposes" of the UN, which include inter alia the prevention and removal of threats to the peace, international cooperation in solving global economic and humanitarian problems, and respect for human rights. A UN member cannot threaten or use force against the political independence of any other state (Article 2[4]), and the UN cannot intervene in matters "which are essentially within the domestic jurisdiction of any state"(Article 2[7]) *except for* UNSC-authorized enforcement measures under Chapter VII.

JUS AD BELLUM

Left open to interpretation, however, is what constitutes a threat to international peace and stability, and who decides. The post–cold war era has hurtled these issues into dramatic relief: is a state free to do harm to its own citizens so long as it does not attack its neighbors, or does the international community have a responsibility to react for humanitarian purposes? Although the UNSC is to determine under Article 39 a "threat to the peace," it has been argued that the development of humanitarian law now places gross violations of human rights and crimes against humanity as not falling exclusively within the "internal affairs" of a state. Also, "While a 'threat to the peace' has historically been taken to mean a military threat to other countries, advocates maintain that in certain cases of extreme suffering or abuses of human rights" the term should have a broader meaning, just as it was used to justify UN sanctions against Rhodesia and South Africa, and that perhaps the UN Charter should be amended or another international convention be adopted to define the conditions and authority for humanitarian intervention without the consent of the state concerned.[2]

It is against this backdrop that the legitimacy of Allied Force, conducted without UNSC authority, must be measured.

On the one hand, Russia and Yugoslavia denounced the operation as violating the UN Charter. Russia suspended its relationship with NATO and cooperation with the United States in nuclear risk reduction. Foreign Minister Yevgeni Primakov declared "We must not set a precedent for NATO to act outside its area without the consent of the UN Security Council, where Russia wields a veto."[3] By the end of 1999, Defense Minister Igor Sergeyev even proclaimed, reacting to Western criticism of Russian military actions in Chechnya: "Our relations with the alliance have apparently entered a new phase of getting colder. The Alliance is trying to talk to Russia about the problem of Chechnya from a position of force."[4] Being that NATO is led by the United States, in Russia's perspective obviously consenting to Allied Force would have amounted to acknowledging a unilateral American *droit de regard* over international security, regardless of Belgrade's behavior. At the OSCE Istanbul Summit in December 1999, Yeltsin branded NATO's action "aggression" that was "spearheaded" by Washington—the old theme of urging Europe to distance itself from the United States, divide NATO and, of course, attempt to portray itself as an honest member of the European family—all this from a confused nation with such perverse associates as Belarus and Serbia, and one which immediately stepped up cooperation with China after the Founding Act was signed. Moscow Mayor Yuri Luzhkov even stated that attack on Yugoslavia was a testing ground for "possible" measure against Russia itself.

The culprit, the Federal Republic of Yugoslavia (FRY), took the position that the NATO threat of air operations was an "open and clear threat of aggression" against a sovereign state and that Belgrade was threatening no other state. The threat that referred to the Activation Warning, or ACTWARN, was given on September 24, 1998, permitting commanders to identify the assets for both a limited air option and a phased air campaign, and the Activation Order, or ACTORD, was given on October 13, 1998 (on January 30, 1999, the NAC delegated authority to the secretary general to authorize strikes). Belgrade further stated that NATO was violating Article 2[4] of the UN Charter prohibiting, again, the threat or use of force against another state or in any other manner inconsistent with the "Purposes" of the UN, and as a violation of Chapter VIII of the Charter which prohibits regional agencies of the UN from undertaking enforcement action without UNSC authority (Yugoslavia incorrectly described NATO as such a regional agency, which it is *not*).[5] That is, the FRY asserted, as Russia likewise seemed to do, that no one had the right to interfere by other than peaceful means, if any at all, with the work of Mephistopheles, that ethnic cleansing and mass deportations was an internal matter. Paradoxically, Belgrade also argued that UNSC authority had to be given, as if NATO retaliation was no more than a procedural flaw. Perhaps more clever lawyers could have instead or in addition argued that Allied Force constituted unlawful foreign assistance to insurgents in a civil war, with UN General Assembly (UNGA) Resolution 2131 (XX) prohibiting interference in "civil strife in another state."

On the other hand, NATO, confronted with the certainty of a Russian and Chinese veto in the UNSC, justified its actions on various but not apparently coordinated grounds. In announcing on March 23, 1999, his orders to SACEUR to initiate operations, Solana stated:

NATO has fully supported all relevant UN Security Council resolutions, the efforts of the OSCE, and those of the Contact Group. We deeply regret that these efforts did not succeed, due entirely to the intransigence of the FRY Government. . . . We must halt the violence and bring an end to the humanitarian catastrophe now unfolding in Kosovo. . . . We will do what is necessary to bring stability to the region. We must stop an authoritarian regime from repressing its people in Europe at the end of the 20th century. We have a moral duty to do so. The responsibility is on our shoulders and we will fulfill it.

But on whose authority was left ambiguous, evasive, or even irrelevant. The following rationales were given:

- "In support of the goals" of UNSC Resolution (UNSCR) 1199 of September 23, 1998, which termed the situation in Kosovo "a threat to peace and security in the region," but did *not* authorize any military action.[6]
- In response to FRY violations of international law and use of indiscriminate force.[7]
- As a "recognized exception" to UNSC authority in order to avert humanitarian catastrophe, the situation which the NAC cited on January 30, 1999, upon authorizing Solana to authorize air strikes. He claimed: "not to have acted would have meant that the Atlantic Community legitimized ethnic cleansing in its immediate neighborhood."[8] NATO Ambassador Alexander Vershbow suggested the UNSC can be overruled or ignored:

NATO's 19 sovereign nations would, I think, prefer to have such a mandate in every case except Article Five defense. But as we saw in Kosovo, there may be times when an exception is necessary, if one or more permanent members of the Security Council do not live up to their responsibility.[9]

Lord Robertson, as UK defense secretary, informed the House of Commons "Our legal justification rests upon the accepted principle that force may be used in extreme circumstances to avert a humanitarian catastrophe . . . as an exceptional measure in support of purposes laid down by the UN Charter, but without the Council's express authorization."[10] As NATO secretary general, he elaborated:

the decision to use force against Belgrade has been the most controversial one in NATO's history. We knew that NATO would be charged by some with taking the law into its own hands. And we also knew that, especially in those countries that regained their independence only recently, our decision would raise concerns that NATO was undermining the established concept of state sovereignty. . . . And yet we felt we had no choice but to act . . . we had to draw the line. We felt that we had to send the unmistakable message: policies of ethnic cleansing and mass deportation have no place in this Europe of the 21st Century. . . . It was always clear that NATO's actions would constitute the exception from the rule, not an attempt to write new rules. All Allies have a vital interest in a predictable international order. They all cherish their national sovereignty . . . But the specific circumstances of the Kosovo crisis defied traditional categories . . . our decision was totally vindicated by the course of events. Through NATO's actions, ethnic cleansing was not only stopped, but indeed reversed.[11]

- "To stop the violent dismemberment of states"[12] (which could apply to both the Kosovar insurgents seeking independence or the turmoil in neighboring countries brought on by the flood of refugees).

- As what might be interpreted as an application of the inherent right of self- and collective-defense under Article 51 of the UN Charter, such that states should have the autonomous right to defend values and not only their sovereignty and not necessarily requiring a UNSCR, that is, such defense is not an "exception" but stands on its own. In other words, the right of self-defense recognized by Article 51 "if an armed attack occurs" does not mean "if and only if," just as whether the use of force other than against the territorial integrity or political independence of another state is permissible may be debated. In their own words:

Solana: "In responding to the Kosovo crisis, the Alliance has sent a strong signal that it will defend the basic values of the Atlantic community: liberty, democracy, human rights and the rule of law,"[13] and that "NATO must act within the framework of the United Nations but there may be occasions where . . . we will act by consensus if there is an obstacle in the Security Council."[14]

Naumann: there was no "clearly defined common interest" or "clear and present danger" to any ally, and that NATO simply fought for the principle that "human rights ought to be respected."[15]

Vershbow: "Our shared values—freedom, democracy, the rule of law, respect for human rights—are themselves every bit as much defending as is our territory."[16]

Canadian Foreign Minister Lloyd Axworthy: the need exists for "international rules that focus on the security of individuals as opposed to traditional thinking about security of the state,"[17] citing this as doctrine reflected in inter alia the UN Charter, the Universal Declaration of

Human Rights, and the Geneva Conventions and Protocols, and that the NATO action "demonstrated how the defense of human security has become a global concern: it was the humanitarian imperative that galvanized NATO into action."[18]

Cohen: "An ethnic conflict in the immediate neighborhood of NATO members threatens stability in the whole region . . . [a NATO operation] could . . . be collective defense."[19] (Note that Solana also referred to the "immediate neighborhood," but without suggesting longitude or latitude for bounding NATO areas of interest.)

- Whether or not Allied Force was sound policy but bad law is nobody's business but NATO's. U.S. Under Secretary of Defense for Policy Walter B. Slocombe described the NATO Strategic Concept as meaning that "NATO's crisis response activity must be consistent with international law, but significantly [the Strategic Concept] does not suggest that NATO must have permission from the United Nations or any other outside body before it can act. . . . We were successful in making clear that it is the Alliance, and not any other body—the UN, OSCE, PJC [Permanent Joint Council] or whatever—whose decision is required."[20] And Solana stated: "To some extent, we just have to go ahead where there are threats, and we'll work out the theory later."[21] That is, if sound policy must rest on bad or contestable law, then it is the law which needs adaptation, and, if not possible, so be it.

- As, citing Solana, nothing more pure than a "moral duty."

The Strategic Concept reflects broad flexibility. The alliance may engage in crisis management to support the security and stability "of" (not synonymous with "in") "the Euro-Atlantic area" and to do so "in conformity" with the UN Charter. The earlier, 1991 edition of the Strategic Concept had mentioned crisis management, but it was linked to "crises affecting the security of its [NATO] members." Interestingly, whereas the 1991 version declared that "none of its [NATO's] weapons will ever be used except in self-defense," this was *not* repeated in the 1999 issue. Equally permissive are the EU Helsinki Council conclusions of December 10, 1999: "The Union will contribute to international peace and security in accordance with the *principles* of the United Nations Charter" (emphasis added). This is quite unlike the aforementioned Hjelm-Walonen proposal whereby EU "armed peacekeeping actions . . . must be based on a mandate from the United Nations or the . . . OSCE," raising an issue that is no doubt to be revisited.

UN Secretary General Kofi Annan has framed the central dilemma of the emerging interpretation of *jus ad bellum*—the lawfulness of war: "On the one hand, is it legitimate for a regional organization to use force without a UN mandate? On the other, is it permissible to let gross and systematic violations of human rights, with grave humanitarian consequences, continue unchecked?" Viewing the inability of the "international community" to reconcile these views, the secretary general suggested that "it is essential that the international community reach consensus—not only on the principle that massive and systematic violations of human rights must be checked, wherever they take place, but also on ways of deciding what action is necessary, and when, and by whom." He argued that "a new, broader definition of national interest is needed in the new century, which would induce states to find greater unity in the pursuit of common goals and values . . . the collective interest *is* the national interest."[22]

All the same, more questions seem to be raised than answered. The following queries are offered not as mere law school hypotheticals. They do require a response because activities such as Allied Force may not in the future always prove casualty-free, and governments, parliaments, and the public will need to be presented with a sustainable justification for sending forces into harm's way and to ensure that legislatures grant access to rather than deny NATO the means to accomplish the mission:

1. President Clinton declared "We cannot do everything everywhere. But simply because we have different interests in different parts of the world does not mean that we can be indifferent to the destruction of innocents in any part of the world."[23] Yet, both Solana and Robertson referred to the specific case of Kosovo, and both Cohen and Solana referred to the "immediate neighborhood" of NATO. Was the slaughter of nearly one million people in Rwanda of no significance to NATO because it was not in the "immediate neighborhood?"

2. The NATO Strategic Concept does *not* expressly identify defense of values or common interests versus territory as an alliance security task. Ambassador Vershbow did state "we hope the 1999 edition will make clear that NATO is not just defending territory, but defending the common interests of its members,"[24] that "the new Strategic Concept puts a necessary emphasis on defense of common interests and common values," and that "the most significant evolution" from the 1991 to 1999 Concepts is "emphasis on defense of common interests and values."[25] But this is not self-evident from the text, even if that is the U.S. view. "Crisis management" is listed separately from Article 4 "consultation," with that consultation linked to "any issues that affect *their vital interests,* including possible developments posing risks for *members' security*" (emphasis added). Likewise, Washington was unable to secure a provision that NATO could act without a UNSCR, with Secretary Cohen having argued "We should avoid language in the Concept which would require NATO to have a UN or other mandate. All military actions should have an appropriate legal basis and should be decided upon by consensus. . . . Accordingly, the Strategic Concept should provide a permissive framework"[26]—which it does. But President Clinton did certify to Congress on January 31, 2000, that the Concept "imposes no new commitment or obligation on the United States."[27] So where is this "most significant evolution" as opposed to simple recourse to Article 4?

3. The 1999 OSCE Charter for European Security describes as "threats to security" the violation of human rights and fundamental freedoms. Why then did Lord Robertson state that Allied Force "would constitute the exception from the rule" of not undermining sovereignty? What then of NATO's new mission of crisis management?

4. Why can NATO address disorder in a nonmember state, but not within its own members?[28]

5. Can nonstate actors call upon a third party to intervene against the offending state?

6. If legal opinion is divided on whether or not a state can intervene in another state to defend its nationals, surely the issue would be more complex when non-nationals are being defended against the will of the host state.

7. Had NATO forces in the FRY been aggressively attacked, would this have triggered Article 5 as it applies to alliance forces when in "the North Atlantic area north of the Tropic of Cancer" (Article 6)?

8. Does the illegal conduct of the FRY military and police forces justify a response of questionable legality from NATO? Is this, whether or not the "right thing to do" and however imperfect the UN system, simple anarchy?

9. There is no getting around the problem of abuse of precedent. Here a bottomless, slippery slope does indeed arise. For instance, defense of "values" could well have described the repressive "Brezhnev Doctrine" that placed maintaining "socialism" above national sovereignty including by the use of force as an "extraordinary measure," or atrocities such as Tiananmen Square. Hitler cited the interests of Germans in pursuing *Lebensraum* at any price. The 19th century notion of defending "interests" and not just sovereignty is "generally discredited"[29] for obvious reasons in that each state defined for itself what interests it would go to war to defend, even if as a pretext for aggrandizement—although presumably this fault would not arise were a set of democratic and actionable interests agreed, at least among like-minded nations, as jus cogens (peremptory norms which a treaty cannot alter).

10. Would NATO's case have been weakened if UNSCR 1199 had not described the crisis as a "threat to peace and security in the region?" Or is intervention an independent right regardless of UNSCRs?

11. Would the context have been radically different if Belgrade only attacked civilians and combatants outside its territory?

12. Might a Contact Group decision have in theory (as Russia is part) been an acceptable substitute for an enabling UNSCR?

13. It would be an understatement to suggest that not all allies would subscribe to the view that NATO should defend values and interests whenever and wherever. A very senior NATO military officer, requesting anonymity, reflected in early 1998 that collective defense must not be replaced by a notion of the defense of common interests. Collective defense is relatively easy to define while collective interests are undoubtedly not. If for more than forty years NATO has been unable to achieve consensus on the relatively simple concept of an Alliance "Area of Interest" in an easily understood bipolar world environment, "what makes us think we can suddenly achieve a consensus to define the considerably more complex concept of common collective interests in this era of continual change in a multipolar world?"

France, the only Ally not formally integrated into NATO's military structures, has traditionally proved reluctant to see NATO take on missions other than collective defense. Alone of the OSCE participating states, Paris tried to constrain NATO participation in OSCE (it was not until 1999 that a NATO secretary general addressed an OSCE Summit) and, alone among the North Atlantic Cooperation Council (NACC) participants, consistently tried to block NACC real-world peacekeeping with absurd claims that WEU could take on such tasks (which it never did). French President Chirac stated: "If NATO gives itself the right to intervene where it wants and when it wants, other powers would immediately start doing the same thing, with as much justification."[30] French Foreign Minister Védrine argued: "NATO must not be diluted ... NATO cannot be used for everything, everywhere on the pretext that member states have interests" (although this argument would apply equally to WEU or EU operations).[31]

It has also been argued that the new members want the "old NATO" of collective defense, not a crisis management body or a forum for enhanced European responsibility (how could it be otherwise following decades of Soviet repression?).[32]

U.S. Senator Jesse Helms, chairman of the Foreign Relations Committee, has called for NATO to not replace the UN as the world's peacekeeper, build democracy, or promote better relations with Russia; "Rather, NATO's mission today must be the same clear-cut and limited mission it undertook at its inception: to protect the territorial integrity of its members, defend them from external aggression, and prevent the hegemony of any one state in Europe."[33]

Although simply reflecting Article 4 of the Washington Treaty and adopted the year before Allied Force, the U.S. Senate Resolution of Ratification of April 30, 1998, approving the admission of the three former Warsaw Pact states referred to "NATO capacity to project power *when the security of a NATO member is threatened*, and that the core purpose must continue to be collective defense "in order for NATO to serve the security interests of the United States" (emphasis added).

Senator and initial U.S. presidential hopeful John Ashcroft argued that "If we want a global NATO, the treaty should be resubmitted for the Senate's consideration."[34]

14. Kosovo was *not* a pure instance of upholding values. Stopping the humanitarian catastrophe was expressly linked with avoiding destabilization of the Southeast of NATO, preserving NATO credibility, and sustaining the NATO-Russia relationship. According to the Pentagon:

The United States and its NATO allies had three strong interests at stake during the Kosovo crisis.

First, Serb aggression in Kosovo *directly threatened peace throughout the Balkans and the stability of southeastern Europe*. There was no natural boundary to this violence . . . Instability in this region had the potential to exacerbate rivalries between Greece and Turkey, two NATO allies with significant and often distinct interests in Southern Europe.

Second, Belgrad's repression in Kosovo created a *humanitarian crisis* of staggering proportions. . . . NATO and other members of the international community responded to this crisis, preventing starvation and ensuring, ultimately, that the Kosovars could return safely to their homes.

Third, Milosevic's conduct leading up to Operation Allied Force directly challenged the *credibility of NATO* . . . Had NATO not eventually responded to these violations [of agreements to be verified by the KVM and monitored by NATO] . . . its credibility, as well as the credibility of the United States, would have been called into question.[35]

Likewise, Lord Robertson did state that Allied Force was about defending values, but he also stated that "our *strategic interest* in preventing the conflict from spreading *coincided* with our humanitarian interest in stopping ethnic cleansing."[36] None should be maudlin.

15. Although NATO credibility was stressed, the White House took the view that victory would have been won "inside or outside NATO. . . . We want to move with NATO, but it can't prevent us from moving,"[37] despite the fixation with NATO "unity of purpose" during the campaign.

16. What values warrant military intervention to protect? War crimes and repression seem obvious, but may not be as clear-cut as news accounts portray, witness the exaggerated accounts of Kosovar casualties at the hands of the Serbs. What if ethnic cleansing does not entail murders? What about torture? Racism? A rigged election? Drugs? Bioterrorists? A maneuver to grant a politician lifetime tenure, as in Turkmenistan? Even though many OSCE states criticized Russia during 1993–1996 and 1999–2000 for using disproportionate force against Chechen insurgents, none proposed intervention as in Bosnia or Kosovo—why not, or does protecting values depend on the relative weakness of the oppressor? How did Allied Force match upholding US "interests"? The Pentagon view falls short of a roadmap but may be the best of all possible worlds as a raw guide for policy:

both U.S. national interests and limited resources argue for the selective use of U.S. forces. Decisions about whether and when to use military forces should be guided, first and foremost, by the U.S. national interests at stake—be they vital, important, or humanitarian in nature—and by whether the costs and risks of a particular military involvement are commensurate with those interests. . . . U.S. national interests include:

- Protecting the sovereignty, territory, and population of the United States.
- Preventing the emergence of hostile regional coalitions or hegemony.

- Ensuring uninhibited access to key markets, energy supplies, and strategic resources.

- Deterring and, if necessary, defeating aggression against U.S. allies and friends.

- Ensuring freedom of the seas, airways, and space, as well as the security of vital lines of communication.

In other cases, the interests at stake may be important but not vital—that is, they do not affect the nation's survival but do significantly affect the national well-being and the character of the world in which Americans live. . . . Such uses of the military will be both selective and limited, reflecting the relative saliency of the U.S. interests involved.

When the interests at stake are primarily humanitarian in nature, the decision to commit U.S. military forces will depend on the magnitude of the suffering, the ability of U.S. military forces to alleviate this suffering, and the expected cost to the United States both in terms of American lives and matériel, and in terms of limitations on the United States' ability to respond to other crises. Military forces will be committed only if other means have been exhausted or are judged inadequate.

In all cases where the commitment of U.S. forces is considered, determining whether the associated costs and risks are commensurate with the U.S. interests at stake is central. Such decisions also require identification of a clear mission, the desired end state of the situation, and a strategy for withdrawal once goals are achieved.[38]

Another classification goes as follows, but it too does not come with instructions:

Tier one (vital): homeland defense, to include threats to the well-being and way of life of the American people

Tier two (strategic): peace and stability in Europe and Northeast Asia, open access to energy supplies in the Middle East

Tier three (lesser): stability in South Asia, Latin America, and Africa; the spread of open markets favorable to U.S. prosperity [39]

So, was Allied Force, if not intended to advance a vital interest, either "important" or "humanitarian"? Can one truly conclude that a year after the operation that an "end state" has even been defined (UNSCR 1244 spoke only of "an interim political framework")? Is defense of values under violent threat an "important" interest in itself or "primarily humanitarian"? What conflict does not affect the character of "the world in which Americans live," which presumably must stand for more than secure trade and safe tourism? Would NATO have acted earlier in Bosnia if oil was at stake, or would the Europeans have acted in much the same way as they did in the buildup and prosecution of Desert Storm against Iraq? Yes to Kosovo, no to the Southern Hemisphere? (For example, then–U.S. presidential candidate in the 2000 race George W. Bush took the view that U.S. forces should not intervene in Rwanda.) And even if the administration concluded that a humanitarian crisis warranted intervention, would Congress revisit the debate on each occasion, even trying to invoke war powers?

17. Why should geography matter if NATO is committed to promoting peace, security, and liberty for "all people of Europe and North America"? Would a NATO force in the Caucasus be conceivable given the energy interests in the region, or would that be too removed from what Secretary Cohen termed the "immediate neighborhood" of NATO? If a secure oil and gas pipeline route from the region to the West that avoids crossing Russian territory is a U.S. national security interest, would Washington and its allies take action to secure that energy flow, as they did against Iraq? If not, why? Because the region is recognized as Russia's sphere of influence?

18. Might the regional interests of allies in having stable neighbors generate more caution in considering a NATO operation, as was the case with Hungary not willing to allow its land territory to be used to support troop movements to the Balkans during Allied Force? Would France wish to see NATO engaged in its former colonies in Africa? Would the German Bundestag have approved a German-led Allied Force against World War II adversary Yugoslavia?

19. Because future operations will likely be conducted with non-NATO nations, it would seem desirable to have the principle of humanitarian intervention or defense of values accepted at the widest possible level. The natural framework would be the OSCE, which in theory unites like-minded states committed to democracy as the *only* form of government. However, the OSCE, as discussed in chapter 7, has excluded enforcement action from its array of possibilities, and has never conducted the peacekeeping missions that were agreed in 1992. The United States takes the view that if it was to participate in peacekeeping, this would most likely have to be under NATO, even though an OSCE-led operation would have the advantage of Russia being an equal participant and not a guest. This could also prove a crippling drawback, as witnessed by Russian obstructionism prior to and during Allied Force, but at least it would present states with organizational choices and an opportunity to test OSCE procedures.

20. NATO's justification for Allied Force does not necessarily square with its arrangements with partners, who, again, will most likely join the allies in future PSOs. The NATO-Russia Founding Act speaks of joint operations "under the authority of the UN Security Council or the responsibility of the OSCE" (although also stating that any actions undertaken by NATO or Russia together or separately "must be consistent with the UN Charter"). And in 1993, the NACC ministers agreed that peacekeeping could only be carried out under the authority of the UNSC or OSCE, which NATO rejects, viewing (at least in the U.S. perspective) a NATO-led operation as a sine qua non for PSOs in or around Europe (although there is no reason why such a mission could not be undertaken under OSCE authority, not command or control).

21. Whether in defense of values or security interests, did the means match NATO's goals of ending the violence in Kosovo and assure: the unconditional return of all refugees and internally displaced persons; withdrawal from Kosovo of Yugoslav military, police, and paramilitary forces (which was not required under the earlier Rambouillet texts not accepted by the Belgrade authorities); unhindered access by humanitarian aid organizations, a secure environment; and establishment of a political framework for Kosovo recognizing Serbia's territorial integrity? Yes, the alliance assembled 900 aircraft from 366 at the outset, and flew over 38,000 sorties over 78 days with no casualties and only two aircraft lost to hostile action (an F-117 and F-16). More than 23,000 weapons were delivered with a minimum of collateral damage—the "most precise and lowest collateral-damage air campaign in history."[40] Yet, the U.S. European Command itself acknowledged that "Achieving Alliance consensus in gaining approval during this operation complicated our efforts. . . . As commanders, of course we would have wanted to conduct a more rapid, overwhelming campaign with more strike power."[41] Senator John Warner took a more critical view:

Of particular interest to this Senator are the NATO decisions not to even allow the planning for a ground option, and the decision to go with an incremental, gradually escalated bombing campaign. With these two decisions, NATO abandoned the principles of using all assets at a commander's disposal, and striking fast with overwhelming forces. We will be debating the fallout from these decisions for years to come. Instead of achieving the goal as stated by President Clinton on March 24 [1999], 'to protect thousands of innocent people in Kosovo from a mounting military offensive,' NATO's initial bombing runs were followed up by an increased campaign of death and destruction by Milosevic's forces. Would the outcome have been different if NATO had moved sooner and more decisively—including with the threat or prepositioning of ground troops? NATO military leaders struggled under the constraints dictated by the need to preserve alliance unity—from the graduated pace of the air campaign, to the prohibition on the use of ground troops, to the need to have individual targets approved by political authorities [micromanaged by the five principal Allies, or "quint"] in a number of allied nations. Did we pay too high a price to achieve consensus among the 19 allies?[42]

Subsequently, Senator Warner questioned what, beyond stopping the massacre, had been accomplished: "What has the coalition achieved? Unacceptable, dangerous levels of criminal activity continue, and put our troops at constant risk. Precious little other progress has taken place in Kosovo." If the president could not certify that the Europeans were meeting their commitments, he would call for the phased withdrawal of U.S. soldiers.[43] As a legislator, the senator did, as always, have the cost-free luxury of calling for a perfect world, zero American body bags, and pristine exit strategies. Indeed, in the postwar phase, KFOR troop levels were (at the beginning of 2000) not a few hundred or thousand, but 12,000 below the pledged level of

49,000. Inexperienced units were replacing tested peacekeepers. KFOR troops were compelled to take up tasks normally within the responsibility of the police (with the UN falling 2,000 short of its pledged police contribution). De facto partition of Kosovo, split through Mitrovica perhaps, may be inevitable, and that would hardly be unique in the world, but that was not the outcome NATO claimed to seek to prevent.

22. Is the U.S. fixation with safety, to the extent that U.S. KFOR troops commonly withdrew from potential Serb-Kosovar Albanian confrontations, and a de facto preference to leave the "bleeding" to the Europeans compatible with non-Article 5 missions that define the new NATO?

23. If humanitarian intervention is an exception to UNSC-sanctioned missions, why did NATO cite the purposes and the spirit of the Charter and UNSCR 1199? What if 1199 had not been adopted?

24. Could not the legal principle of "choice of the lesser evil" as a principle of justification for the use of force sufficed?

25. Were at least some NATO members more interested in fragmenting the residue of Yugoslavia and destabilizing Milosevic than in undertaking humanitarian intervention and inducing political settlement (as might be suggested by the absence of any Dayton-like framework for a peace settlement, and the de facto annexation of Kosovo by NATO under UN auspices)?

26. Would it have made a difference in law if NATO had not chosen to "degrade and disrupt" Serbian forces but instead simply deployed ground forces to separate the warring parties even without Belgrade's or Moscow's consent, with robust rules of engagement to avoid a repeat of the massacre in July 1995 of the so-called safe area of Srebrenica in Bosnia as UNPROFOR peacekeepers stood aside?

27. If a principal goal was to check spillover, could not preventive deployments as the UN Preventive Deployment Force in Macedonia (UNPREDEP) have served the goal?

28. Was the non-negotiable NATO proposal offered to Serbia at the 1999 Rambouillet talks, which Milosevic rejected, truly an appropriate exhaustion of all peaceful means to resolve the crisis?

29. NATO asserted, if not articulating well, that Allied Force was based on a belief that it was in accordance with international law, that is, opinio iuris. However, the majority of authoritative legal scholars argue that there is no such principle of humanitarian intervention, that state practice does *not* support the argument that such a principle does exist, and that no post-conflict UNSCR provided retroactive legitimacy.

30. Lastly, as there was no consolidated NATO legal position, it has been urged that NATO should articulate such a rationale: "in whatever way the NATO action may be explained, as deviating from the law, as conforming to the law, or as progressively developing the law, the international community has so far not received a clear answer," and NATO should have made use of the 1950 "Uniting for Peace" mechanism whereby a two-thirds majority of the UN General Assembly can assume responsibility for international peace and security when the UNSC cannot do so. "In the interest of the progressive development of international law, NATO and/or its member states should take part in this process by enunciating a doctrine on humanitarian intervention, in an objective attempt to make sense of the past for the benefit of the future."[44] Above all, the UN Charter should never again prove a source of reassurance to perpetrators of atrocities.[45]

FOR A NEW CONTAINMENT

The question, then, of what is worth sending men and women of the armed forces into harm's way and where, remains just that. As the preceding rationales for Allied Force show, it can be debated whether NATO was acting for values, interests, indirect defense, prowess, or some combination—"we'll work out the theory later." But NATO has raised expectations without any commitment to act. This could encourage both the oppressor and the oppressed, but that is also the case with the UNSC. This ambiguity about how NATO might respond, however, might nevertheless promote deterrence of conflict and crimes against humanity at the outset since NATO remains, after all, the only credible collective defense and security organization. "Potential adversaries learned that NATO may no longer regard claims of sovereignty as a shield against Allied intervention in their affairs," even if "NATO may be more likely to take decisive action to protect interests near Europe, than when interests at a greater distance are affected," and run the risk that states concerned about NATO "interference" may develop WMD as a deterrent.[46] But despite the difficult questions raised supra, surely it is not beyond the grasp of intelligent life on earth to assure that atrocities of the type witnessed in the Balkans are *not* within the exclusive competence of the state hosting such slaughters and deprivation. Devising the best range of methods to do so in itself must be considered a NATO "fundamental task." Otherwise, we are simply doomed to repeat the past.

4

RUSSIA

And where do you fly to, Russia? Answer me! . . . She doesn't answer. The carriage bells break into an enchanted tinkling, the air is torn to shreads and turns into wind; everything on earth flashes past, and, casting worried, sidelong glances, other nations and countries step out of her way.[1]

Nikolai Gogol
1842

The Russian Federation's national interests in the international sphere require the implementation of an active foreign policy course aimed at consolidating Russia's positions as a great power and one of the influential centers of the developing multipolar world. The main components of this course are . . . the development of equal partnership with the other great powers, the centers of economic and military might.[2]

National Security Blueprint of the Russian Federation
December 17, 1997

The challenge of helping Russia become a normal European country, integrated into the family of Western democracies, is as formidable today as it was a decade ago. . . . If Russia wants to be a player in the post-Cold War European security system, it has to stay engaged with the institution [NATO] that—like it or not—will remain the central pillar of that system.[3]

U.S. NATO Ambassador Alexander Vershbow
November 8, 1999

> We believe we can talk about more profound integration with NATO,
> but only if Russia is regarded as an equal partner.[4]
>
> Acting Russian President Vladimir V. Putin
> February 29, 2000

During the long period of East-West confrontation, NATO as an organization abjured official contacts with the USSR and other members of the Warsaw Pact. Despite U.S.-Soviet détente and West German *Ostpolitik*
beginning in the latter 1960s, NATO HQ was strictly off-limits to officials
from Warsaw Pact nations, and any outside contacts (embassy reception
persiflage, seminar discussions) had to be reported (by both sides). Although NATO and the Warsaw Pact acted as blocs in conventional arms
control negotiations since 1973, the 1990 CFE (Conventional Forces in Europe) Treaty was signed by the individual states and limitations applied not
to two alliances, but to the absurd political fiction of two "groups of states."
Indeed, many in NATO seemed not to feel as vanquishers, but alarmed that
the Warsaw Pact was dissolving, because of generic concerns about "stability" or the impact on NATO's existence; they would have perhaps preferred
a "reformed" pact or a neutral zone for Central and Eastern Europe (CEE)
between Germany and Russia. Arms controllers were peeved because the
geopolitical seachange in Europe could disrupt the tidy CFE limits and in-
spection quota procedures—as if the West would have preferred to have
Soviet shock armies poised along the German-Polish frontier (and the med-
als for a pact campaign in the West had already been struck). Moreover,
NATO did not want to equate itself with the coerced Warsaw Pact, such that
when in May 1988 the East proposed interalliance political contacts, it was
ignored. Savants such as Henry Kissinger viewed in 1990 neutrality as the
most realistic system for Central Europe, whereas Zbigniew Brzezinski argued the year before that dissolution of the two alliances could lead to
anarchy.

But these rules of nonengagement simply reflected the grim reality:
when political reforms stirred in CEE, the Free World was "intent on respecting the basic rule of the cold war: 'Don't cross the East/West demarca-
tion line.' "[5] Indeed, when Warsaw Pact troops occupied Czechoslovakia in
August 1968, NATO was instructed not to go on the alert, even though there
were concerns that independent Yugoslavia might be affected.

On June 7–8, 1990, however, the NAC judged that the time was ripe to
"extend to the Soviet Union and to all other European countries the hand of
friendship and cooperation," as they declared at Turnberry, the United
Kingdom. In the London Declaration of July 5–6 that same year, the NATO
heads of state or government declared: "The Atlantic Community must
reach out to the countries of the East that were our adversaries in the Cold
War," and NATO offered to invite the governments to establish regular diplomatic liaison "to share with them our thinking in this historic period of

change" and to intensify military contacts (which had been taking place since 1975 in the CSCE under the rubric of confidence-building measures, and naturally before that bilaterally). The USSR established diplomatic liaison with NATO and later, Russia and all the other former Soviet republics, including the Central Asian states which made no pretense of being new democracies joining the consultative North Atlantic Cooperation Council (NACC) created in 1991 at U.S. and German initiative, but neither Presidents Gorbachev nor Yeltsin ever addressed the NAC as did other heads of state or government from the East (if only perhaps a matter of form—why should a head of state or government play guest to ambassadors or even foreign ministers?).

When the NATO PFP program was announced at the January 1994 Brussels Summit, Russia sought in addition to conclude a special arrangement "virtually as between Allies" to recognize what the crippled state sought to promote as the image of a Great Power (*derzhava*). President Yeltsin had already proposed in mid-September 1993 a NATO-Russia treaty as an alternative to NATO enlargement to the East, calling for NATO-Russia relations to be "warmer" than those between NATO and Central Europe. NATO had never formally differentiated among the NACC participants, some of whom sought precisely that, because they sought not seminars but NATO membership. The alliance had stated on May 29–30, 1989, at a Brussels Summit that "each country [in the East] is unique and must be treated on its own merits," just as the United States had traditionally pursued a differentiation policy toward those Warsaw Pact members who differed in their policies from Moscow, primarily Romania. The only exception was during the supposed coup attempt against Gorbachev, when the NAC declared on August 21, 1991, that "The illegitimate actions currently have negative effect on the Alliance's relationship with that country," that "We expect the Soviet Union to respect the integrity and security of all states in Europe," that NATO's liaison arrangements with "the Central and Eastern European democracies now take on added significance," and that "we reiterate our conviction that our own security is inseparably linked to that of all other states in Europe, particularly to that of the emerging democracies"—language which a NATO source stated was intended to signal the coup leaders that NATO would "keep our options open."[6]

Yet, NATO agreed to apply differentiation to Russia, and not without consternation to those NATO aspirants who had always been sensitive to a "Russia first" policy assigned to the Clinton administration and thus felt that their aspirations would be placed on hold depending on what Russia agreed with NATO, and who were cautious of the secretive nature of the NATO-Russia negotiations (the first appearance of the agreement occurred because of a press leak to Reuters). The first step was agreed on June 22, 1994, in the form of a "Summary of Conclusions of Discussions between the

NAC and Foreign Minister of Russia Andrei Kozyrev" (Russia had preferred the simpler term "protocol," but there were supposedly linguistic differences that would have implied something more formal than NATO chose). The rather lamely-entitled "Summary" pledged development of a "far-reaching, cooperative NATO/Russia relationship" focusing on information exchange (to demonstrate the "new NATO"), political consultations, and cooperation in security-related areas including peacekeeping "as appropriate."

A year later, on May 31, 1995, this was elaborated in an "Areas of Pursuance" document, and Russia concluded its Individual Partnership Program (IPP) with NATO and agreed to participate in IFOR. But Russia did not respond to a NATO proposal of September 26, 1995, for a "Political Framework for NATO-Russia Relations," as it preferred a legal document which NATO claimed it could not conclude as an organization (a position not undisputed within NATO itself, and there was nothing to prevent the then sixteen allies and Russia to sign such a document, although it was argued that the possible complications of ratification by the Duma should be avoided). Following more than a year and a half of contention and theatrics over NATO enlargement, the result was the "Founding Act on Mutual Relations, Cooperation and Security between NATO and the Russian Federation," signed in Paris on May 17, 1997.[7]

Two days after the Founding Act was signed, NATO initialled a "Charter" on a "distinctive partnership" with Ukraine at the latter's insistence.[8] Although Ukraine had renounced after debate its share of the former Soviet nuclear arsenal, and could be viewed as either a little Russia or a big Poland, NATO acquiesced so as to support Ukraine's independence. For if Ukraine, plagued by corruption, an anti-reform parliament, possible tensions in the Russian-speaking sectors of the country including the Crimea (one-fifth of the Ukraine's citizens), and unclear as to its foreign policy orientation, returned to the Russian sphere of influence, then the military calculations of NATO enlargement would have to be revised (Ukraine shares a border with allies Hungary and Poland and with potential allies Slovakia and Romania). The "distinctive partnership" fell short, however, of the security guarantees neutral Ukraine believed NATO should extend to it. (A tentative effort by Belarus, which unlike Ukraine had yet to at least begin steps towards reform and accept, as did Ukraine, NATO enlargement as "directed at enhancing the stability of Europe," according to the NATO-Ukraine Charter, to do the same with NATO was ignored because of a perceived illegitimacy of the government of Alyak Lukashenka.) Ukraine in 1997 was the first to open a NATO information center supported by the Alliance, an institution which Moscow resisted for itself however (positive or negative depending on the audience) such a modest step would be.

The NATO-Russia Founding Act established a Permanent Joint Council (PJC) meeting monthly among ambassadors and annually at the level of foreign and defense ministers. Consultations and cooperation covered nineteen areas, ranging from discussions about security and stability in the Euro-Atlantic area to joint operations and "possible cooperation" in theater missile defense. This was largely a repackaging of the PFP work program, although the PFP Framework Document proviso (paragraph 8) that NATO will consult with any active partner if that partner perceives a direct threat to its territorial integrity, political independence, or security is amended such that NATO and Russia will consult in case one of the PJC members perceives such a threat (thus making the NATO-Russia Act more similar to Article 4 of the Washington Treaty whereby "The Parties will consult together whenever, in the opinion of any one of them, the territorial integrity, political independence or security of any of the Parties is threatened"—vs. the NATO+1 notion of the PFP plus the requirement of the partner being "active").

Critics variously argued that NATO had allowed Russia too close to its inner workings and equated the NAC with the PJC; that the act was an attempt to establish U.S.-Russia "condominion" over Europe to the detriment of ESDI (as a number of French officials and parliamentarians suggested); that as a defensive alliance, NATO should not have concluded an agreement with any particular country; and that the act was a humiliating Yeltsin "capitulation" comparable to the Versailles Treaty, simply a face-saving political favor to Yeltsin with no real substance. They argued further that establishing the PJC as an institutional mechanism for partnership to "coordinate" the foreign and defense policies of Russia and the West was "more important than NATO enlargement because if Russian and NATO military machines and foreign policy are complementary, not competitive, the security of Europe is ensured"; and that given Russia's weakness, the act was a "great achievement" by making Russia "a full participant in European decisionmaking on security issues."[9]

However, the act specifically excluded consultations about "internal matters of either NATO, NATO member States or Russia." The intent was to establish a relationship of "no vetoes, no surprises." This seemed naïve but necessary. The act held political significance in that Russia was recognizing NATO as a partner and vice versa, but by way of substance the June 17, 1993 "Charter for American-Russian Partnership and Friendship" had already called for unified efforts to prevent and settle regional conflicts, create "a credible Euro-Atlantic peacekeeping capability," and develop "ballistic missile defense capabilities and technologies" (despite concerns about Russia's nuclear cooperation with Iran).

With the act in hand, NATO then brought a parallel outreach track to fruition by inviting on July 8, 1997, three former Warsaw Pact member states to join NATO by the time of the fiftieth anniversary of the alliance in 1999—a target that was known well before by the three. Upon entering the alliance, these three nations—the Czech Republic, Hungary, and Poland—could add fourteen divisions and twenty combat air squadrons, an increase of about 25 percent and 20 percent, respectively, albeit regulated by arms control agreements. Russia naturally denied that the act was linked to or compensation for acquiescence to limited NATO enlargement, but surely if objections had been that absolute, the act would never have been concluded—even if historians still must make their own judgments about whether "Gorbachev could never have brought the Red Army home had Russia's military believed its bases would be occupied by NATO troops."[10] All the same, in its first six months, the PJC met twice at foreign minister, once at defense minister, and once at chiefs-of-staff level, in addition to the ambassadorial gatherings.

DISTANT FRIENDS?

Dire warnings within and outside Russia about Russia's reaction to NATO enlargement—"countermeasures," forcing the moribund CIS to become a true military alliance, reassessing relations with the West—proved false or at least premature, and the way Russia develops could very well influence the tempo, geographic reach, and military conditions of further NATO widening. Nevertheless, although a principal aim on NATO's part (despite its limited public diplomacy structure always wedded to "good news," and with some staff not even aware that the then current Strategic Concept still referred to a potential threat coming from the Soviet Union) was to reassure Russia that NATO was not a threat or a tool of German revanchism, a 1997 statement by a commission of the 250 or so members of the "Anti-NATO Group" in the 450-seat Duma asserted:

not later than by 2000 the USA is planning to spread its political and military control over the oil-rich regions of the Caucasus mountains, Central Asia and the Caspian Sea . . . plans are being made to prevent transportation of oil through the pipeline Baku-Grozny-Novorossisjk and to develop the Georgian route (Baku-Supsa [on the Black Sea]) as the only line of export of the 'early' Caspian oil. The next stage is transportation of the 'grand flow' of oil from the Azerbaijan and Kazakhstan sectors directly from Baku to Turkey through territories controlled by Armenia and the Nagorny Karabakh republic and deployment in this region of NATO troops (primarily American and Turkish) under the pretext of 'peacekeeping' in the Armenian-Azerbaijani conflict.[11]

Although this might be dismissed as "red-brown hysteria" for largely domestic political consumption, the predictable tactics of seeking foreign enemies to excuse internal failure to avert Russia's slide towards the Third World, this may become a hot-button issue. Then–U.S. Secretary of Energy Bill Richardson described an agreement concluded on November 17, 1999, for a pipeline bypassing Russia as "not just another oil and gas deal, and this is not just another pipeline. It is a strategic framework that advances American's national security interests"[12]—meaning that the United States would deploy armed forces to protect those interests? The year before, Azeri officials had publicly raised the prospect of inviting U.S. and Turkish forces to be stationed in Azerbaijan to balance Russian influence in (and suspected substantial arms transfers to) Armenia. Georgian President Eduard Shevardnadze had raised the prospect of applying to NATO by 2005, whereas his foreign minister Irakli Menagarishuili stated on September 26, 2000 that NATO was the "main military and political guarantor of stability and security" in the Euro-Atlantic Space, including the South Caucasus. Although this "patriotic" line of a primarily Russian sphere of interest is commonly attributed to then Foreign Minister Yevgeni Primakov, who took office in January 1997, the 1992 Russian Foreign Policy Concept under then pro-Western and subsequently much maligned Foreign Minister Andrei Kozyrev had already warned that the United States might try to replace Russia in the countries of Russia's traditional influence on the pretext of mediating and peacekeeping—even though two years later the Russian military held out the prospect in its special partnership proposals to NATO of "possible interaction during peacekeeping operations carried out by Russia in the former USSR."[13]

Hence, even though Lord Robertson stated in Tbilisi, Georgia, on September 26, 2000, that there could be no regional stability in the caucasus without the participation of the region's major powers "including, of course, Russia" such reassurances (or rather affirmations of reality) compete with the view that through PFP and enlargement NATO is meddling in Russia's zones of special interest with the nefarious aim of gradually "encircling" Russia.

Moreover, PFP exercises in former Soviet republics are regarded with suspicion, with the Duma having sounded an alarm on September 16, 1997, over the exercise the Central Asian Batallion CENTRAZBAT in Kazakhstan and Uzbekistan—even though Russian forces participated alongside their Danish, Turkish, and US counterparts. Communist Crimean politicians called for armed resistance to a NATO exercise held in Ukraine in July 1997, Sea Breeze, the land segment of which was moved from Crimea to Odessa. The Russian Foreign Ministry expressed irritation when the Georgia, Ukraine, Uzbekistan, Azerbaijan, Moldova (GUUAM) regional organization (a balance to the CIS) was established *in Washington* during the NATO anniversary summit, which Russia refused to attend. On April 21, 2000, Kazakhstan, Kyrgyzstan, Uzbekistan, and Tajikistan—all PFP states—concluded a defense and security pact, supposedly what the CIS was to have been.

Russian officials continue to suggest that NATO should become a "political/peacekeeping organization" as part of a new system of European security coordinated by the OSCE, and sought to have the NACC and then the successor Euro-Atlantic Partnership Council (EAPC) not so directly linked to NATO, but rather exist as distinct fora. Although it was argued in the West that NATO's new emphasis on defending "values" would actually reassure Russia that NATO had moved beyond its original purpose of containment, the 1999 Strategic Concept was criticized by the Foreign Ministry as "in essence a direct claim for a dominant role by the alliance in Europe and world politics [that] does not comply with the interests of stability in Europe and the international commitments undertaken by NATO's member states."[14] President Yeltsin characterized the United States as an "uncle from outside" and called for Europeans themselves to look after their own security (with Russia being among that community),[15] and some high-ranking Duma deputies continue to argue for the withdrawal of US forces in Europe—even though then Soviet Defense Minister Yevgeni Shaposhnikov, referring to Desert Storm, observed on September 18, 1991, that NATO was "a sort of factor of stabilization in the world."[16] And, of course, there always arose the perennial question during encounters with Russian politicians and academics: "Against whom [*protif kavo*] does NATO exist?"

It is not surprising, therefore, that aside from cooperating with NATO forces in Bosnia and Kosovo, Russia has not proved an "active" partner despite the language of the Founding Act about a "fundamental new relationship between NATO and Russia" aimed at developing "a strong, stable and enduring partnership." It has been slow to establish an agreed NATO military liaison mission in Moscow while enjoying political and military presence at NATO and SHAPE, and it was not until 1998 that Russian ground forces took part in a PFP exercise—Cooperative Jaguar in Denmark. Why the Russian military is said to have opposed making the NATO-Russia work plan public is a matter of speculation: perhaps because it treated it as serious military business, or because it would not sit well politically with various forces in Russia (for those officers who did participate in PFP activities were said to have not promoted their careers). General Naumann described the PJC as attesting to "de facto recognition by Russians that NATO is, and will remain, the cornerstone of security in Europe for the future,"[17] but Yeltsin argued that "the concept of 'NATO-centrism,' and manifestations of it, such as expansion of the alliance, remains unacceptable to Russia."[18] By expanding eastward, NATO would "considerably" decrease "the buffer zone" between NATO and the Russian Federation, use of newly-acquired airfields would provide NATO with "a possibility of delivering a major surprise aviation strike at targets in the Russian Federation," use of Polish ports "will considerably impair the freedom of movement of the Russian Baltic Fleet," and revive "the long-buried confrontation between Catholic-Protestant and Orthodox countries in Europe."[19]

The persistent theme that NATO is not treating Russia as an equal but as a junior partner if not a plain nuisance to be pampered, is not just a purported Russian argument. According to a U.S. Congressional Research Service report:

although the NATO-Russia Founding Act and the Permanent Joint Council create the veneer of treating Russia and NATO as equals, in reality, NATO does not regard or treat Russia as its equal. As the Kosovo conflict continued, it further damaged already strained relations between NATO and Russia. On one side, years of NATO efforts to convince Moscow that the alliance was not a military threat to its security were undermined [NATO could not say that it was strictly "defensive," even if offensive actions were taken to "defend values," and, as noted, the 1999 Strategic Concept does *not* state as before that NATO will not be the first to use force]. On the other side, western concerns about Russian intentions and reliability were reinforced.[20]

Allied Force created a schism, the aftershock of which has yet to be measured. On the day the operation began, Yeltsin charged that NATO had "violated" both the UN Charter and the NATO-Russia Founding Act, creating a "dangerous precedent" for the "rebirth of a policy of forcible diktat." The NATO Secretary General received a faxed letter from the Permanent Delegation of the Russian Federal Assembly to the consultative NATO Parliamentary Assembly repeating these assertions, charging that the operation "cannot but be characterized as a dangerous precedent in world politics fraught with consequences, which are indeed destructive for international peace and stability." Yeltsin suspended, but did not abrogate, the PJC and participation in the EAPC on March 26, year when a Russian-sponsored UNSCR demanding an immediate halt to NATO action was defeated by an overwhelming twelve votes. Russia provided Serbia with radar data on the flight paths of NATO aircraft. On April 2, Foreign Minister Igor Ivanov even ascribed NATO's motive as being the dismemberment of Yugoslavia (even though no NATO nation supported independence for Kosovo, even if that may be the ultimate consequence of KFOR and UNMIK). The Russian media tended to parrot the Serb line of blaming the refugee crisis of a million and a half individuals on the NATO bombings rather than the policies of Milosevic, and drew parallels between Chechnya and Kosovo. Liberal Party Chairman Vladimir Zhirinovsky asked whether autonomous NATO action would not justify Russia deciding itself on how to support ethnic Russians in Estonia and Latvia.

Then, on June 12, after Allied Force came to an end, some 200 Russian troops in Bosnia painted the "KFOR" logo on their vehicles and raced to the airport in Pristina, Serbia, twelve hours before NATO forces entered Kosovo (a deployment which Russian military authorities claimed had not been notified to them and thus was a "provocation"). The Russian troops, without even combat service support and without having notified the SFOR commander, then blocked NATO forces from entering the base which was to have possibly served as KFOR HQ. An order by SACEUR to dislodge the Russians was not carried out by the responsible British subordinate commander following consultations with London (a procedure informally known as playing "the red card"). Foreign Minister Ivanov immediately described the Russian deployment as a "mistake," but no withdrawal order followed. Within days, however, an agreement was reached on June 18 whereby Russian forces would be deployed to the French, German, and U.S. KFOR sectors, and the PJC resumed in July albeit limited to KFOR issues. Still, later in the year, Russian Duma deputies approached the prosecutor of the International Criminal Tribunal for the Former Yugoslavia (ICTY) to determine whether NATO had committed war crimes in Kosovo, (prosecutor Carla del Ponte concluded on June 13, 2000 there was no basis to open a criminal investigation, although the ICTY has no jurisdiction to question the legality of the use of force). And on January 10, 2000, a national strategy document was signed by Acting President Vladimir Putin describing NATO's decision to use force outside NATO borders as "a threat of destabilization of the whole strategic situation in the world." There was no mention of "partnership," but instead only "cooperation." Military readiness was described as "critically low," requiring if all other means have been exhausted, the use of nuclear arms, and was interpreted as conveying a view of the West as a competitor interested in ensuring Russia's weakness.[21] Defense Minister Igor Sergeyev stated "Our relations with the alliance have apparently entered a new phase of getting colder," and that NATO was trying to talk to Russia about Chechnya "from a position of force."[22]

Two years after the signing of the act, Ambassador Vershbow, an experienced analyst of Russian politics, gave an address in Moscow with the telling title of "Promise of Partnership or Problems." He assessed Russian participation in the PJC as "often reduced to simple catch-phrases or slogans" and "quick tabulations of short-term benefits." He believed that Russia had made two important mistakes: supporting Milosevic in his argument that no international military force was required to enforce a political settlement in Kosovo, and suspending PJC participation, with the PJC having been intended as "an all-weather institution."[23] SACEUR reportedly has viewed too many Russian officers at NATO as more interested in intelligence than building partnership,[24] and invariably the limited Russian participation in IFOR, SFOR, and KFOR was not divorced from observing NATO procedures (which Russia copied, within its more limited means, during Russia's renewed campaign against Chechen rebels in 1999–2000). So there is, perhaps, still an element of infiltration rather than partnership mentality, and Kremlinology has certainly outlived the Soviet Union.

It is, of course, highly important to heed the advice that "it is not hard to see why Russian analysts and nationalists," however absurd or hysterical their views may seem to foreigners, "worry that their country's influence on the Baltic and the Black Seas, in the Caspian basin, in the South Caucasus and even Central Asia might soon be greatly curtailed, even to the point of exclusion,[25] because of Western political and economic interests. At the same time, only Russia can answer the question of why her friends are hard to come by.

PERSISTENT ENGAGEMENT

There will probably always be a degree of friction between NATO and Russia as Moscow seeks to reestablish its place on the world stage and break out of a Soviet-era trance. When, in the legendary poet Aleksandr Pushkin's words, "the shadows are no more" is but a matter of sheer speculation. In part, this is inevitable by virtue of the Founding Act itself: on the one hand, the act commits both sides to consult and inform each other on steps they are planning to take concerning security in the Euro-Atlantic area; on the other, consultations are not to extend to "internal matters." Yet, obviously NATO non-Article 5 missions or alliance enlargement are not purely "internal matters," just as the West does not regard Chechnya as solely an internal Russian affair. Moreover, even if not adversaries, both parties must take the other into account in their military planning, thus placing a limit on how far military cooperation can go (sharing intelligence and arms technology?), whereas collaboration in the south of the former USSR might be perceived as anti-Islam. NATO still regards Russia as a residual "risk," and a possible "near peer" competitor posing a nuclear and conventional threat—although the Strategic Concept does not state that in so many words. There is also the view that "Since Russia cannot accept the legitimacy of other central European states' interests in formulating its own policies, it cannot play a large role in Europe, a consideration that eludes but does not trouble Russian policymakers. Moscow craves status, not responsibility, in Europe."[26] Russia did, of course, acquiesce in NATO's initial enlargement to CEE, but surely the case of former Soviet republics will be a test, as discussed in chapter 5.

Nevertheless, sight must never be lost of the big picture. Despite the inability after ten years to adopt the essential laws to regulate transition, contain the tradition of corruption in Russia, enhance quality of life, and overcome Soviet-era mentalities as quickly as was done elsewhere in the former Warsaw Pact, Boris Yeltsin still proved the first freely-elected president of Russia. Never in its history has Russia enjoyed so many years of freedom however chaotic, and all ex-Soviet troops have been withdrawn from Central Europe, including the Baltic States. The PJC should not be seen as a payoff for NATO enlargement or a token to appease Moscow. Although it may be true, as then U.S. deputy assistant secretary of defense, the late Joseph Kruzel, put it to one of the coauthors in June 1994, that "A great power does not have to go around telling everyone it is not Albania," it is truer still, as then German Defense Minister Volker Rühe stated the month before: "NATO cannot treat Russia as Tajikistan or Albania."

Beyond the historic cooperation in IFOR/SFOR/KFOR with NATO, the relationship has also extended to air defense, when in 1998, Russian transport aircraft loaded NATO radar and missiles in two exercises. The United States would like to pursue discussion of strategy and doctrine, WMD, counterterrorism, theater missile defense, early warning, regional security problems, combined peace support operations, military-industrial cooperation such as in strategic airlift, and retrain military personnel and convert industries to peaceful uses. NATO has taken the extra step of limiting the peacetime military arrangements on the territories of new allies. The 1997 U.S. idea, which apparently did not garner interest on either side, for a NATO-Russia brigade (first suggested earlier that year by NATO International Secretariat member Nick Williams) should be reactivated as an important confidence-building measure, particularly given the proliferation of such units among NATO and non-NATO nations (e.g., between Poland and Ukraine, Poland and Lithuania, Hungary and Romania, among Italy, Hungary, and Slovenia, and among the three Baltic Republics, or the Black Sea Naval Cooperation Task Group). A common air and ground defense system would be another important sign of goodwill. Apparent German-Russian agreement in 1999 to upgrade the Soviet era Mikoyan-Gurevich aircraft (MiGs) of Poland, Hungary, Slovakia, Bulgaria, and Romania to NATO standards (e.g., increased range, upgraded navigation aids, the ability to distinguish friendly from enemy aircraft), and Russian ambitions to market the An-7X as the "Future Large Aircraft" for European militaries however financially motivated, may be politically significant beyond the business dimension, for, intuitively, if Russia viewed these states as a threat, why arm them? And surely sterile PJC communiqués should be re-examined as to what public diplomacy they might have in preaching to the unconverted.

Fortunately, the potential for a fresh start presented itself officially on February 16, 2000, when a joint NATO-Russia statement was issued in Moscow committing the sides to "work to intensifty their dialogue" in the PJC, to make their cooperation "a cornerstone of European security." Acting president of the Russian Federation Putin stated: "we believe we can talk about more profound integration with NATO, but only if Russia is regarded as an equal partner," and even answered the question of whether Russia would join NATO: "Why not?" (a response Gorbachev and Yeltsin had also made in the past, albeit referring to an unspecific changed alliance).[27] For the record, Lord Robertson responded that although Russian membership was not on the agenda "right now," "Mr. Putin's views reflect Russia's interest in engaging in a strong relationship with NATO, and are very promising for the future."[28] That will depend on the imagination of both sides. The world will not change whether or not START II is ratified or START III negotiated, and Washington and its allies must look beyond the narrow if still relevant arms control dimension to sow the seeds for a comprehensive relationship so as, to cite the Founding Act: "to contribute to the establishment in Europe of common and comprehensive security based on the allegiance to shared values, commitments and norms of behavior in the interests of all states." That remains the great prize, and the question of whether or not Russia may eventually join NATO need not be answered for the medium-term future, nor is that the most important issue.

In the final analysis, Henry Kissinger has offered this *Realpolitik* perspective on what is in effect an extension of the 1967 NATO "détente plus defense" formula:

At the end of the Napoleonic wars France was in the position Russia is in today, that is, it was considered to be the aggressor in Europe. Everybody was deeply concerned about the fact that they might start on expansion again. So they created two separate institutions. One was the Quadruple Alliance . . . aimed at preventing a military attack from France. Second they created something called the Concert of Europe in which France could participate [and the Concert was "the last time that Russia shared responsibility with other great powers in designing the architecture of an undivided Europe"[29]]. The Concert of Europe discussed all the political issues, and in fact that became in time the dominant element. The Quadruple Alliance was never abolished, but it never needed to be activated.

This is sort of the model that I have in mind for Russia. I think Russia should be consulted and participate in political discussions that affect its vital interests and the peace, and that as Russia evolves those institutions become more and more dominant. But I would keep NATO as a safety, and keep it as unspoiled as possible as a community of democratic nations.[30]

5

THE OPEN DOOR

To encourage the nations of Central and Eastern Europe to organize themselves as a barrier against Russia would be to make a commitment that the United States could not carry out.[1]

Walter Lippmann
1943

The Parties may, by unanimous agreement, invite any other European state in a position to further the principles of this Treaty and to contribute to the security of the North Atlantic area to accede to this Treaty.

Article Ten
The North Atlantic Treaty

[O]ne must suppose that if any of the Eastern European countries was suddenly to emancipate itself from the Soviet tutelage and to require that a new place be found for it in the European scheme of things, the Western NATO powers would be no less appalled by such a development than the leaders of the Soviet Union.[2]

George F. Kennan
1977

The prospect of NATO expansion to the East is unacceptable to Russia since it represents a threat to its national security.[3]

National Security Blueprint of the Russian Federation
December 17, 1997

Security is the basis for reconciliation, in which Russia's neighbors, weaker than Russia and smaller than Russia, also feel secure.[4]

Zbigniew Brzezinski
May 26, 1998

It is simplicity itself.

Sherlock Holmes (Sir Arthur Conan Doyle)
"A Scandal in Bohemia"
1891

Few NATO issues seemed as controversial as the decision to enlarge to the East.[5] At the January 10–11, 1994 NATO summit in Brussels, the sixteen leaders declared: "We expect and would welcome NATO expansion that would reach to democratic states to our East, as part of an evolutionary process, taking into account political and security developments in the whole of Europe." Unlike the prior admissions of Greece and Turkey in 1952, West Germany in 1955, and Spain in 1982, NATO was expanding ("enlarging" or "widening," to be politically correct) to its former adversaries of the Warsaw Pact. Despite persistent Russian opposition to NATO enlargement, similar to Soviet objections to a united Germany in NATO, at the alliance Madrid summit on July 8–9, 1997, the Czech Republic, Hungary, and Poland were invited to join. All but three of the allies supported, if rather late in the game, German support for Slovenia and French advocacy of Romanian membership. But given the June 1997 U.S. decision to support only three candidates, the other allies went along with the consensus rather than defer a decision.

The Protocols of Accession were then concluded on December 16, 1997. Following a relatively smooth ratification process, admission occurred on March 12, 1999. This was well in time for the Washington anniversary summit when the allies hoped to admit the three as new allies, reflecting a relatively short timetable made known to the three at least a year before to reassure especially a suspicious Poland that its NATO membership would not somehow be held hostage to the vicissitudes of the NATO-Russia relationship.

From the time of the Madrid decision, NATO declared that it would keep its door open, and that no state would be excluded because of geography, in principle including Russia. Yet, the "how," "when," and "to whom" are still not completely clear, and will certainly prove a continuing challenge, as well as a historic opportunity for the alliance to widen itself with like-minded nations while working with all European countries in partnership. The answers are integrally related to the future of the alliance itself: what kind of organization is enlarging and for what purpose? And if there is some natural limit to enlargement, then should NATO still exist?

THE ROAD TO MADRID

In a sense, NATO's first enlargement to the East already occurred when Germany was united on October 3, 1990. Unlike the case with other NATO allies, the USSR had a voice because of the post–World War II Four Power arrangements (together with France, the United Kingdom, and the United States). The Soviet Union at first called for a neutral Germany, one belonging to *both* NATO and the Warsaw Pact, or holding the issue in abeyance until both alliances had been dissolved, and the Social Democratic Party in the Federal Republic was opposed to early unification and a united Germany in NATO. In the end, however, Germany entered as a full NATO member subject only to the legal stipulations of the "2 + 4" Treaty on the Final Settlement on Germany that no foreign forces or nuclear weapons would be stationed on the territory of the former German Democratic Republic (Article 5), but Germany would nonetheless enjoy "all the rights and duties" arising from the right of the united Germany to belong to an alliance, a right which "is not affected by this Treaty" (Article 6)—suggesting non-deployment was conditioned upon the strategic environment.

Had Gorbachev, whose political survival was paramount in Bush administration calculations, insisted, a neutral Germany might instead have been the result. According to former President George Bush, "an unattached Germany on the loose in Central Europe may have looked to him worse than one embedded in NATO," but that "the outcome was not at all foreordained."[6] It is disputed whether any promises were made to Moscow during the "2 + 4" negotiations regarding Germany that NATO would not again enlarge to the East,[7] and U.S. Secretary of State James Baker did state that "there would be no extension of NATO's current jurisdiction."[8] However, the fact is that no verbal record exists of any agreement to this effect, and even as Germany was uniting, the Pentagon was already examining further enlargement.[9] By early 1992, the United States was publicly suggesting that very future.

Secretary General Wörner, said to be somewhat "ahead of the curve," stated on September 10, 1993: "Even if there are no immediate plans to enlarge NATO, such a move would increase the stability of the whole of Europe and be in the interest of all nations, including Russia and Ukraine. Nobody will be isolated."[10] He was responding to the continued efforts of the new democracies of Central and Eastern Europe to rejoin Europe, viewing membership in both NATO and the EU as the foundation of their security and prospects for prosperity. Indeed, even before the Warsaw Pact formally dissolved on July 1, 1991, following earlier pressures by Hungary (which, in May 1990, proposed negotiations to leave the organization, a step that in 1956 proved disastrous), the three "Visegrad" countries of Czechoslovakia, Hungary, and Poland declared on February 15, 1991, their intention to integrate into "European security structures." On March 11 that year, Bulgarian President Zhelyu Zhelev called for his country's immediate "associate membership" in NATO, given the turmoil in Yugoslavia and the risk of spillover (although the foreign minister of the old-guard Bulgarian government, Boyko Dimitrov, informed one of the coauthors on March 20, 1989, that "We do not regard the basis of a future system of security in Europe as the dissolution of the Warsaw Treaty Organization and the strengthening of NATO.") After war broke out in 1991 in Yugoslavia, Hungary cited the potential threat of Serbian bombing of nuclear plants on Hungarian territory as a justification for NATO security guarantees, with Hungarian diplomats having said that NATO nation diplomats had been telling them that citing a threat would increase Hungary's prospects for NATO membership.

Also in 1993, with a U.S.-proposed alliance summit being planned for later that year or early 1994, NATO diplomats and officials addressed the issue of enlargement. There was a view that it would "not seem timely" to deal with the enlargement question at the summit. But there was also support for sending a signal that NATO was not a closed shop and that enlargement would enhance the stability of all European states, not unlike the arguments for a united Germany integrated into NATO rather than pursuing its own security course, or *Sonderweg*. Alliance brainstorming sessions raised fundamental issues:

- Would NATO evolve from a collective *defense* into a collective *security* organization (i.e., members would be obliged to defend any member against aggression by another member rather than a threat from outside)?

- What might be the impact of NATO admission for some states but not others—would it encourage or discourage reform in those not admitted at an early stage and sharpen ill will between neighbors, such as between Hungary and Romania?

- Should the summit identify the most promising candidates?

- Would EU membership be a better answer for the new democracies, or was that prospect too distant such that NATO was perhaps not the best but the only game in town?

- Should NATO differentiate by bringing in the then likely Visegrad candidates, just as the EU and the WEU had been able to differentiate by building relationships with nations with the perspective of EU membership?

- If the 1992 CIS Tashkent Security Pact could enlarge, why not NATO, an argument Polish Defense Minister Janusz Onyszkiewicz used? Or was this argument too resonant of a past bloc-to-bloc syndrome?

- How could NATO convey to Russia that its intention was not to foster new spheres of influence or dividing lines, but rather stabilize the East?

- How would Article 5 apply to new members from the East—could the model of East Germany prohibiting peacetime stationing of foreign forces and nuclear weapons be applied indefinitely?

- How politically reliable were the former Warsaw Pact states and could they be trusted with military secrets?

- Was enlargement necessary under current conditions as opposed to building partnerships with a broad array of countries? If enlargement was not necessary, then could not the same be said of NATO?

- Should specific guidelines and timetables be offered at the summit, as candidates and some Western politicians demanded, or was Article 10 sufficient?

- Could some form of "associate" or "observer" status be offered in the interim (as the Bush administration suggested in 1990)?

- On balance, was NATO enlargement a positive development for the alliance?[11]

Voices within the U.S. and German governments alone among the allies were sympathetic to enlarging NATO to stabilize a heretofore buffer between Germany and Russia. The reasons were a mix of political and strategic considerations: if reform in Russia were to collapse and a new threat arise, then NATO would, by acting now, acquire greater strategic depth ("We need Poland in NATO to defend Berlin" as German defense planners said); at the same time, Article 10 of the Washington Treaty could not be applied selectively, and there was a moral imperative to enlarge so as a logical consequence of NATO's long-standing efforts within limits to promote positive change in Central and Eastern Europe. Other voices within the same governments saw no reason to start planning for widening, were worried about the effect on relations with Russia and on the cohesion and efficiency of the alliance, or viewed Central and Eastern Europe as an area where Americans had never fought[12] (even though the German invasion of Poland precipitated World War II) and had no strategic interest (despite the vast investment the United States and its allies made to prevent a cold war from heating up). "Russia was invaded many times through Poland" was the cautious view of one NATO official when the debate began in the early 1990s, as if Poland was fated to be a permanent object of Great Power manipulation. The Pentagon and some elements in the State Department were not in favor of any fast track, and were joined by a small cluster of former officials with their formative experience during the cold war and a fixation with nuclear weapons in Russia, as if Armageddon would rain down if NATO enlarged, as well as interest groups voicing concerns about anti-Semitism and property restitution. Opponents found a receptive home with the *New York Times* (which had supported the Yalta pact effectively ceding Soviet occupied lands to Moscow's control) and the supporters in the *Washington Post*.

And it was a recurrent theme both in the United States and abroad that President Clinton and pro-NATO enlargement supporters in the Congress (who were in the majority following the 1994 Republican takeover of both Houses) were simply seeking the ethnic vote, noting that Clinton had called in a 1996 campaign speech in a Polish suburb of Detroit for invitations to be issued, but though the majority of U.S. public opinion favored widening NATO. Likewise, it was insinuated that the United States was simply seeking new markets for its defense industries, but that would not require membership, whereas if large corporations on either side of the Atlantic thought they would cash in, they were surely disappointed as all three had postponed major weapons modernization programs.

But perhaps most chilling to the aspirants was the view that if "Russia's neighbors become the targets of Moscow's renewed expansionary ambition, and if these neighbors had developed close relationships with the West and its organizations, then we could see a return to tension, even perhaps an element of confrontation"[13]—as if a wait-and-see attitude would deter new-Soviet adventurism more so than by acting on the principle of Article 10 and the longstanding CSCE/OSCE principle that states are free to choose or change their security arrangements, or that Russia would be better off with anxious neighbors. Even as late as 1993, NATO was reluctant to take up Central European offers to make their impressive training areas available to NATO nations because it was felt that, at least in the UK view, "too close cooperation could harm NATO-Russia relations and draw NATO into unstable regions" (although, as a practical matter, NATO exercises in Western Europe carried social consequences even during the Cold War, with, for example, Autumn Forge-84 causing property damages on the order of nearly $1 million, throughout Europe). After PFP was announced in 1994, these concerns gave way and the first PFP exercise was help in Poland (in September of that year), Cooperative Bridge, and NATO nation forces did avail themselves of such training grounds in part because of the popular sentiment in the West against disruptive large-scale maneuvers and noisy air training.

President Clinton is said to have come to the conclusion following a discussion with Polish and Hungarian leaders at the Holocaust Memorial ceremony in Washington on April 23, 1993, that the question of new NATO members was not one of whether, but when. But it was really German Defense Minister Rühe who pushed the envelope since that same year, and it was not until the 1996 election year that the president is believed to have made the decision to *implement* the policy (indeed, according to sources, the U.S. National Security Council staff were not confident until 1996 that the president would not change his mind). However, the theory that enlargement was driven by trying to create an issue for American election politics is not validated, not only because public opinion as a whole favored enlargement, but because Republican presidential candidate Bob Dole also favored enlargement—with the 1994 Republican "Contract with America" having favored a wider NATO.

True, administration rhetoric at times appeared to contrast a decision on NATO enlargement with the striving for a peaceful order throughout Europe. One State Department official testified on February 1, 1994: NATO should not "foreclose the best possible future for Europe: a democratic Russia committed to and working with and for the security of all its European neighbors. . . . But, at the same time, [PFP] preserves the means to deal with a darker future, should it occur."[14] Whereas, U.S. NATO Ambassador Robert Hunter would argue that "none of the aspirants for joining NATO are really threatened now"[15]—as if the threat element was a factor at least as to the timing of widening, which was, if true, hardly plausible: why would NATO enlarge given Russian opposition when the sun was not shining? Such a step would hardly promote crisis stability, and could even make the case for suspending NATO itself. However, President Clinton eventually stopped referring to not creating new "dividing lines" (which, as Senator Richard Lugar pointed out, could be read to imply that NATO would not enlarge by definition) in favor of no "veils of indifference," and in the end, U.S. leadership was decisive.

A few months prior to the Madrid summit, then–NATO assistant secretary general for political affairs, Ambassador Gebhard von Moltke, assessed the alliance approach as follows:

The major impetus for opening up the Alliance comes from Central and Eastern Europe itself. These countries have made a very strong case for becoming part of a European and Euro-Atlantic integration process from which they were artificially separated for decades. They want to join the Atlantic community NATO represents and enjoy the stability our countries have enjoyed for decades. We have no right to keep them out. All OSCE-states have recognized in several documents the sovereign right of each state to freely choose its security arrangements, including membership in an Alliance. NATO's policy is guided by the aim to widen the zone of stability in Europe without creating new dividing lines. We have therefore taken a careful, considered approach and set the enlargement process in a network of wide cooperation embracing all interested European countries, including Russia.

Why is the inclusion of new members extending stability and the zone of stability in Europe? NATO has not only provided the member countries with the conditions to develop their political and economic structures in a stable way but also to stabilize the relations among the member countries. And it does so until this very day. The process of preparation for membership in the Euro-Atlantic institutions is already exerting a powerful influence on the development of the countries who aim at joining. With the incentive of possible NATO membership clearly established, virtually all the countries interested in joining have speeded up their democratic reforms and their move towards market economies and settled old disputes with their neighbors. . . . None of this would have happened so quickly without the firm commitment of the Allies to open the Alliance to new members. . . .

In order to ensure that the opening of NATO increases security and stability for *all* of Europe, not just those who join the Alliance, we will have to take into account the needs of those who do not join or who may join later. This will require NATO remaining open for further accessions and for building trust and close cooperation with all interested European countries . . . a European security architecture worth its name must be one that gives Russia its rightful place and makes it part of the development of such an architecture . . . Russian perceptions do matter and have to be taken seriously. Continuing Russian anxieties are based on a profound misunderstanding of NATO's character and intentions. All the more reason, therefore, to make a special effort to allay those fears and remove the misunderstandings. But this cannot be done—and will not be done—at the expense of other European countries and their interests.[16]

Also prior to Madrid, NATO had made nonlegally binding NATO pledges to Russia, although it is not recorded in the Protocols of Accession, that the alliance would not station nuclear weapons or substantial conventional forces on the territory of new members in peacetime. In addition, although the 1999 adapted CFE Treaty leaves Russia at a 1:3 disadvantage via NATO in main battle tanks—the reverse of what the Warsaw Pact/NATO balance had been ten years before (assuming such a "balance" is valid for military planners to make), it does restrict ground equipment (but not aircraft) temporarily deployed to the territory of another state at the level of inter alia 153 main battle tanks (2 divisions) and 459 main battle tanks in "exceptional circumstances." Russian territory east of the Urals is not affected (although neither is the continental United States or Canada). The three, plus Russia (regarding the Kaliningrad and Pskov *oblasti*), Belarus, Germany, Slovakia, and Ukraine also undertook to either not take full advantage of their treaty equipment entitlements or not request upward revisions. Russian concerns about changes in infrastructure, which NATO will rely on for reinforcement, can be addressed through both the verification provisions of the CFE Treaty and the OSCE Confidence- and Security-Building Measures (CSBMs) regime. Thus, the Pentagon assessed on December 9, 1999, that "NATO Allies addressed deeply-held Russian concerns by accepting provisions in CFE which demonstrated that NATO did not contemplate a massive eastward shift in peacetime military potential as a result of enlargement." That is, at least in peacetime, NATO was extending *stability* and not an Eastern *front*.

HANGING MATTERS

In the U.S. view, NATO enlargement will:

- Expand the region where wars do not happen (because of the security guarantee and because new members are expected to be good neighbors)

- Strengthen the alliance
- Bolster democratic institutions
- "Right the wrongs of the past"
- Promote the business climate.[17]

Table 5-1
NATO Enlargement Military Considerations

- Implications of Collective Defense Security Guarantee
- Ability to Contribute to Core Functions and New Missions
- Accessibility to Territory for Exercises, Reinforcement, etc.
- Pursuit of Interoperability Objectives, Standardization and Multinational Training
- Infrastructure Requirements

Table 5-2
Focus of Pre-Accession Military Work

Near-Term

- Education and Training in NATO Doctrine, Training, and Command and Control
- Establish Interoperable Communications
- Identify Infrastructure Needs
- Identify Requirements for Integrated Air Defense
- Continued Support of Enhanced PFP Initiatives

Long-Term

- Participation in NATO Staffs, Command and Force Structures
- Further Improvements in Interoperability
- Involvement in Defense and Force Planning Processes
- Continued Modernization and Military Reform

Source: NATO Military Committee briefing slides, 1997.

In military terms, although 60 million people were added as NATO shareholders in 1999, NATO's strategic depth was significantly increased by 300,000 square miles and NATO gained a nearly one-fourth increase in ground force capability. According to Pentagon estimates, Poland ranks sixth from the top among the nineteen allies in combat power, comparable to the United Kingdom, with Hungary in tenth and the Czech Republic in twelfth place (some believe the latter two countries may turn out to be "free riders," but that is a very relative evaluation within NATO). All three will need to increase defense spending, modernize, reeducate officers, increase noncommissioned officer ranks, and enhance interoperability, but much of this is no different than what NATO is asking of its older members. Although having prepared to wage war in a confrontational East-West environment but from the other side, the three are not entirely dissimilar from other European allies in terms of what must be done to adapt the alliance. In the absence of a threat, and given existing NATO conventional and nuclear forces, such adaptations may prove politically controversial, but so too will be the case with other allies. And let it be recalled that, unlike the three new allies, Iceland has no armed forces, Luxembourg's are miniscule, and France has still not rejoined NATO's integrated military structure.

In political terms, in view of their post–World War II history, these nations obviously have a special contribution to make in NATO outreach and the special partnership with Russia. Furthermore, by making good on pledges to enlarge to the East, NATO in effect signalled that although it would pursue partnership with Russia, it would not provide safe haven to those seeking to reconstitute the USSR or a Russian sphere of decisive, involuntary control between it and Germany.

In approaching future enlargement decisions, a number of important questions need to be asked which, again, are integrally related to NATO's future as a whole.

First, although NATO insists the open door applies to any qualified state regardless of geographic location, former U.S. NATO Ambassador Hunter has written that among the calculations in inviting the Madrid three was (with the exception of Hungary which had nonetheless provided important support for IFOR/SFOR) precisely their location "on the direct strategic line between NATO and Russia."[18] Likewise, a Slovenian parliamentarian argues the case for his nation by noting that membership would provide not only a land connection between Hungary and another ally but a link along NATO's "strategic corridor number 5 (Barcelona-Kyiv)."[19] So if geography *does* matter, is position along the East-West axis the controlling factor? If so, then the case for Baltic membership should be far less complicated than it seems to be. Or, if the South is the area of greatest danger (the Balkans, the Southern Mediterranean Basin, the Caucasus, Southwest Asia), then should NATO be considering different geography in the future? If enlargement is intended to prevent wars, why not start in the Balkans, where NATO fired its first-ever shots in anger?

Second, although NATO states that enlargement is directed against no one, that it is the East moving West and not NATO moving East, Russia is still considered a risk. Indeed, initial U.S. Congressional Budget Office estimates for the first enlargement were based on an implausible but worst-case scenario: defending against Russia. From a Russian perspective, therefore, the enlargement of NATO *is* aimed at Russia, and it is capability and not intentions that ultimately count. Moscow argues that admission of any former Soviet republics would cross a "red line" because

NATO's borders would further extend eastward to Russia's frontiers. Yet, why can Poland and Norway but not Estonia—or Ukraine—be NATO members sharing a frontier with Russia?

Third, it was argued even before the 1994 NATO Brussels summit that "the easiest way to explain" NATO enlargement to Russia was the need to maintain balance between ESDI and the European pillar of NATO, such that if a state was a candidate for EU membership so too should it also be considered a candidate for NATO membership, and Russia had never objected to EU enlargement (no doubt because it correctly perceived that Western Europe on its own would not be a security challenge). Senator Patrick Moynihan attempted but failed to secure a condition to the Resolution of Ratification that new NATO members should be EU members, which would conveniently postpone further alliance enlargement. However, this so-called "Royal Road" approach had never been applied to any other NATO member, and, of course, Canada, Iceland, Norway, Turkey, and the United States are not EU members, whereas Austria, Ireland, Sweden, and Switzerland are not NATO members. However, might the increased attention to greater sharing of the transatlantic security burden impose such EU-NATO parallelism in future—with the 1995 *Study on NATO Enlargement* having described NATO and EU membership as an autonomous but "mutually supportive and parallel process" (the Baltic states, Bulgaria, Romania, and Slovakia joined in 2000 the accession talks the EU began in 1998 with the Czech Republic, Estonia, Hungary, Poland, and Slovenia—only three of which are NATO members). It has been argued, for example, that EU membership for the Baltic states would mean that "Russia would be less likely to seek to intimidate an EU member out of concern for economic or financial retaliation by the EU, a measure that could lead to overall improvement of Russian-Baltic state relations and, eventually, to Baltic state membership in NATO."[20] Yet, the argument has also been made that the best way to stabilize Russia's relations with Estonia and Latvia would be NATO membership for them, although unlike the case between Greece and Turkey there is obviously no risk of the Baltic states waging war on Russia.

Fourth, was the decision to invite only three nations for the time being a deliberate effort to suggest that countries such as Slovenia and Romania, and then possibly Slovakia and Bulgaria, would constitute the next waves so as to defer the issue of membership for the three Baltic states? Whether or not NATO enlargement includes the task of hedging against a new threat from Russia, why is Baltic membership considered "madness" by many commentators?

Fifth, although, unlike the legally-binding 2 + 4 Treaty, NATO unilaterally stated it has no reason, intention, or plan to station substantial combat forces on new members' territory or store nuclear weapons, does this suggest a second-class status for new members inasmuch as these conditions are not at the request of the new member but by NATO fiat? Why is "getting there" through reinforcement sufficient as opposed to "being there"? Militarily, it makes little difference if a cruise missile was launched from Poland or Norway or offshore but the existence of intercontinental-range systems did not obviate the continued political requirement for the US presence *in* Europe to which even France had never opposed. Although the *Study on NATO Enlargement* raised the issue of whether redeployment or prepositioning would not only be expensive but "could give a misleading impression of Alliance concerns," arms control arrangements have already been concluded to avoid a buildup of military forces in Central Europe. So why are stationed U.S. forces required to demonstrate commitment to European security save in the former Warsaw Pact zone? And would crisis stability be served by a rush through former East Germany to assume forward defense/counter-concentration? Moreover, by agreeing to these limitations, even if not legally binding, did not NATO suggest that it existed to balance Russia?

Lastly, as Russian concerns were a factor in announcing that NATO would enlarge and in the decision to invite the three countries at Madrid, would they not be even more so in considering candidates closer to Russia? If so, will there ever be a good time to enlarge again? Why did Ambassador Vershbow, who foresees new invitations in 2001 or 2002, state on January 20, 2000, that "Despite current strains in our relations with Russia it would be a strategic mistake to pull back from NATO enlargement"? [21] Why link the two? Who seeks to "pull back"?

Hence, the cryptic formula of new members having to meet the general political and military membership criteria (admittedly somewhat of a double standard because NATO does not want to import the kind of frictions and tensions that continue to exist between Greece and Turkey, even though their NATO membership is said to contain their disputes), must also satisfy the strategic interests of the *alliance and* enhance *overall European security and stability*—guidelines broad enough to cover any argument, pro or con.

NATO agreed in Washington to review the enlargement process no later than 2002. The Nordic NATO countries and Poland will lobby for one or more of the Baltic states. The southern allies will support their southern neighbors. Zbigniew Brzezinski, the architect of the dual-track of NATO enlargement plus NATO-Russia partnership, argues that the next enlargement should include at least one country from the North (Lithuania is considered the first) and one or more from the South, and argues that by not closing the door to eventual Russian membership (and President Clinton did not close that door), Moscow's objections will lose force. However, after the Washington summit there was a perceptible dampening of the pre-Madrid agitation for additional invitations, and Congress seemed to have lost interest in the subject.

Of course, security in a crisis does not necessarily mean being a NATO member. Responding to Central European requests for an affirmation that NATO was concerned about their security, the NAC declared in Copenhagen on June 6–7, 1991:

Our own security is inseparably linked to that of all other states in Europe. The consolidation and preservation throughout the continent of democratic societies and their freedom from any form of coercion or intimidation are therefore of direct and material concern to us . . . we will neither seek unilateral advantage from the changed situation in Europe nor threaten the legitimate interests of any state.

Lord Robertson has stated that "NATO can . . . help provide the benign security environment Ukraine needs to concentrate on its domestic reforms."[22] Recall also that NATO extended security guarantees to seven non-NATO states neighboring Yugoslavia should NATO activities on their territory lead to risks to host states. However arguably fantastic politically and militarily under those circumstances and given NATO conventional force shortcomings even against Serbia, this means that *Article 5 can be applied to nonmembers as a precaution*. There is no reason why NATO could not do the same for any country given its declaration that the freedom of democratic societies throughout Europe from coercion is of "direct and material" concern to the alliance. Deploying forces for crisis management would extend the most objectionable NATO dimension from Russia's perspective, *even without any question of membership for the state(s) concerned*. Then–Secretary of State Madeleine Albright has stated that were a "major threat to the security" of the region "between the Baltic and Black seas" to arise, "we would want to act, enlargement or no enlargement,"[23] whereas Senator John Warner declared that "in case Lithuania's sovereignty were ever challenged and NATO did not respond, the Alliance would have lost its purposes—it does not matter at all whether Lithuania is a member of NATO or not"[24]—however, such statements may resonate of the West's failure to defend Poland in 1939 and subsequent Soviet interventions in its "allies."

Moscow's insistence on drawing a line at ex-Soviet frontiers could backfire by promoting calls for NATO enlargement to them to escape what Russia feels is its sphere of "special responsibility." Certainly, given their expropriation from Europe and enchainment by the USSR, the attraction of NATO and EU membership for the Baltic states will not be deferred by rather bizarre suggestions, such as Finland's notion of building a "political security system" with Estonia based on national defense and no Finnish military guarantees,[25] or former British Foreign Secretary Douglas Hurd's suggestion that the Nordic countries could offer security guarantees to the Baltic states in lieu of NATO membership on the grounds that the neutral had been free riders of the alliance during the cold war.[26] This, of course, raises the issue of whether NATO enlargement is necessary to provide security when other means are available, but why should new members who have done so much to end the cold war be denied the same relative certainty of security and the other benefits of full alliance membership? What Polish government would have preferred the risk of repeating the failure in 1939 of France and Great Britain to come to its aid upon the German invasion?

FIRST PRINCIPLES

Looking ahead, much may depend on:

- How the reform of the alliance proceeds. Some may wish to determine how DCI and ESDI are faring, for example, before enlarging again. Moreover, NATO is arguably no longer a purely defensive alliance: how might that affect the attitudes of candidates, with public support for NATO membership in Slovakia having decreased to a mere 35 percent because of Allied Force?

- The course of NATO-Russia relations (although it was Allied Force and not enlargement that caused the 1999 rupture). Enlargement is not supposed to be threat-driven: for example, President Clinton stated on July 7, 1994, that "expansion will *not* depend upon the appearance of a new threat in Europe."[27] Realism compels acknowledgement, nonetheless, of the element of hedging against but not provoking a potential future Russian threat as obviously very much alive. This Russia focus may not only dissuade allies from enhancing their reinforcement capabilities for both Article 5 and non-Article 5 tasks, but by definition prompt Moscow to demand leverage regarding NATO decisions.

- How the new allies are, militarily, advancing their integration into NATO structures, participating in NATO missions, and maintaining commitments to increase defense expenditures (only Poland has a good record), and, politically, endeavoring, as being among the most pro-American states in Europe, to extend the transatlantic community to states left out of the first round of enlargement (all are doing so).[28]

- The mood in Congress. The Senate approved the Madrid invitees by 80:19 votes, but an amendment by Senator Warner, opposed to NATO enlargement, calling for a mandatory three-year pause before the next invitations not only garnered forty-one votes, but is effectively expressed in the Washington summit decision to review the enlargement no later—and possibly no earlier—than 2002. Romanian Foreign Minister Petre Roman saw in early 2000 the dynamics of enlargement politics in the United States as "flat," and future candidates will be "more closely scrutinized" envisages Congressional Research Service analyst Paul Gallis. It should be noted that apart from the Polish American Congress, no other CEE state is as strongly represented in the halls of Congress, and none have done much to rectify this situation, even if it may not be dispositive.

- Possibly the attitude towards NATO membership of the neutral EU members, including Austria and Finland (the latter which has officially not ruled out NATO membership). If the concern is avoiding overload of NATO with states still in transition and experiencing difficulty in modernizing their armed forces, then this problem would not exist for the neutrals and could argue for deferring the new democracies.

NATO's own positions suggest that future enlargement may not prove straightforward and based primarily if not solely on the qualifications of the candidate nation. The Membership Action Plan (MAP), announced at the Washington summit to assist candidates, should provide them with feedback on the specific economic, defense, resource, security (information protection), and legal aspects of membership (Romania was the first to submit its plan, on September 27, 1999). However, MAP is no guarantee of admission, even if the candidate meets the general criteria, and could be seen, as the PFP was conceived, as a delaying action; moreover, the "intensified dialogue" NATO launched in 1996 with states aspiring to NATO membership was supposed to have served the MAP purpose but obviously fell short, and as *demandeurs* may feel disinclined to criticize MAP inadequacies. Those who seek to install a gate at the "open door" could grasp at the slightest obstacle the Madrid invitees may confront in integrating with NATO and proving themselves as security producers to argue for postponement, regardless of the qualifications of candidates.

Yet, MAP and the concurrent "Enhanced and More Operational Partnership" (EMOP) are not the only game in town. A leading Polish parliamentarian observed in 1997 that "Relationships with some of our Western partners (i.e., the United States and Germany) have already acquired the quality of a quasi alliance, and are in many cases of a more profound nature than the Alliance itself," describing the intensified dialogue as insufficiently effective because of "a limited mandate of the NATO team"[29] (one result being the transfer of Corps LANDJUT among Denmark, Germany, and Poland to Szczecin, Poland—which under the prior command structure would have made it a fourth-level NATO HQ). Bilateral and multinational military-to-military collaboration will have an important role, such as the innovative U.S. National Guard Program, the State Partnership Program (SPP), a component of the U.S. European Command Joint Contact Program that twins a U.S. state with a partner country (e.g., Tennessee-Bulgaria, North Carolina-Moldova), and those NATO Members who routinely "support" future candidates should take advantage of the window of opportunity.

Looking ahead, there is no good reason why new countries should not be invited when both parties agree and on the individual merits, not in predetermined groups, arbitrary dates for invitation and admission, or only upon the occasion of a summit. As for what, apart from the candidate's qualifications, will serve the interests of the alliance and Europe as a whole, as NATO requires, would seem to be self-evident if NATO is truly interested in enlarging a community of like-minded nations able to work together in common security challenges and projecting stability to their neighbors. And postponement could very well prove an important, if not the decisive, factor should reforms lose momentum and OSCE commitments be progressively disregarded in candidate states. The West, and certainly the United States with its special role in the alliance, cannot afford to assume this risk.

6

THE HAND OF FRIENDSHIP

We still are committed to defend the territory of our member, but
NATO now is the nucleus of a cooperative security structure that aims
to bring all the democracies of Europe into cooperation to solve problems together.[1]

U.S. NATO Ambassador Alexander Vershbow
May 5, 2000

PARTNERSHIP FOR PEACE

When the NACC was established in 1991, no effort was made to differentiate among its participants, and its purpose beyond overcoming Cold War
insecurity residuals was never very clear. All the same, countries had CSCE
in which to discuss security issues. The NATO-centric basis of NACC had
its own virtue, but there was also a view that participation by the European
neutral countries should be discouraged as this might compete with and
distract from the CSCE. NACC may also have been, or came to be, simply a
way to reassure Russia. Although the relative contribution of Soviet peres-
troika (restructuring) and Western perseverance to the end of East-West
confrontation may be debated, none in the West sought to be perceived as a
victor or conqueror dictating terms to the former Warsaw Pact.

NACC may also have been a device to fend off growing calls in Central
and Eastern Europe (CEE) to join NATO, as suggested by the remarks of a
senior NATO official stated in 1993: "NACC partners *do not need to become
members of NATO* to benefit from the security and stability that it provides

... assisting our new partners with the fundamental transformation of their domestic systems and structures in areas of special NATO expertise."[2] Even here, however, a key item on the agenda was peacekeeping, an area in which NATO as an organization had no experience whatsoever, and even then, France traditionally held back on allowing NACC members to conduct even exercises. If the goal had been to reassure CEE short of NATO enlargement, presumably the *full* range of NATO missions should have been on the agenda from the outset, not just peacekeeping.

In any event, at least in Washington, few had any concrete ideas about what NACC should do; perhaps only slightly more even knew what the council was. Not surprisingly, therefore, NACC quickly became bureaucratic make-work, replete with boring statements, including the unfortunate ex-communist tendency to exceed routinely time limits by reading lengthy speeches about goodwill and peace and reciting all their country's problems. Canada and Hungary felt compelled to propose on July 27, 1994, procedural changes to avoid, according to the joint proposal, what "has proved to be for the most part somewhat insipid and not conducive to substantive interchange on key issues." There was no single (let alone ample) NACC budget, dedicated secretariat, or NATO experts on the former Warsaw Pact countries apart from a small cluster of well-intentioned former Soviet hands. And there emerged no real vision statement differentiating NACC from the politico-military dimensions of CSCE, such that it was suspected that the United States was simply trying to enhance its own influence in Europe through NATO instead of the CSCE where it had less dominance. In comparison, at least WEU's "Associate Partners" from CEE had been selected on the basis of their vocation of joining the EU, although these states assigned greater importance to getting closer to NATO (how the EU absorption of WEU might affect attitudes remains to be witnessed, for provisions have been put in place to allow "interested" nonmember states to participate in EU crisis management).

The next step came in 1994 with the PFP. Unlike NACC, it would focus on the individual needs of participating states and adopt a practical military approach, with active partnership to be a consideration in NATO enlargement, although PFP was related to but separate from steps for NATO membership. This connection was not entirely clear, with the NATO international secretariat having produced a list of more than forty questions in late 1993 and devoted "hundreds of hours" to explore such basic questions as whether PFP was a road to NATO membership or a substitute for it (initially it was certainly the latter, with SHAPE specifically tasked around April 1993 to develop a plan "in lieu of NATO membership"). Nevertheless, NATO would consult with an active partner that perceived a risk to its security, and the PFP would move beyond its initial focus on ensuring democratic control of defense forces, peacekeeping on the ground and not just in discussion of "concepts," and cooperative military relations with NATO leading over the longer term to forces better able to operate with NATO members. That is, in addition to a premembership role, PFP could have a preventive diplomacy purpose by addressing possible root causes of tension such as undemocratic military establishments, and assist NATO in undertaking Article 4 missions. Although those seeking NATO membership and a clear idea of when and how that might occur may have been disappointed, the PFP did not turn out, as Senator Richard Lugar had put it in 1993, a "policy for postponement" about enlargement.

And when the three countries were invited at Madrid, the PFP was "enhanced" to involve partners more closely with NATO decision making and planning, make PFP more "operational," move beyond peacekeeping to non-Article 5 missions, create positions for partners at NATO HQs, and provide them with additional advice beyond "interoperability objectives" to an exchange more closely approximating NATO's force planning system. Likewise, when the three were admitted two years later, NATO established the "Enhanced and More Operational Partnership" (EMOP) containing gradual improvements to the original and to keep participating states interested in PFP whether or not they sought NATO membership.

NACC was terminated in 1997 in favor of the EAPC. This largely amounted to an acronym change, and although EAPC began to focus on individual regional security issues through ad hoc working groups on South-eastern Europe and on the Caucasus, that could have been done in the NACC. Neither NACC nor EAPC is an independent decision-making and operational forum. Both focused largely on seminars and consultations sometimes far removed from NATO's purpose, such as science and the environment (producing tomes on inter alia "air pollution modelling" and "advances in rockfill structures"—although NATO Fellowships were financially appreciated by diplomats and scholars from CEE and the NIS). It has been argued that because SHAPE and not NACC played the key role in IFOR, the relevance of NACC was further diminished,[3] whereas Russia did not bother to rejoin the EAPC in 1999 after the suspension in NATO-Russia relations was lifted by Moscow. One EAPC statement declared, without elaboration, that "there is still considerable potential in the Partnership, particularly in the area of crisis management, the better use of the EAPC, and practical cooperation under PFP. . . . Often, the political discussion is not as substantive as it could be."[4]

As of May 2000, there were twenty-six PFP nations (Croatia having joined that month, making it the third former Yugoslav republic after Slovenia and Macedonia to join) and forty-six in the EAPC (the nineteen allies plus twenty-seven non-NATO countries). EAPC serves as the "overarching framework" for an expanded political dimension of partnership, as well as practical military cooperation under PFP. The 2000–2002 Partnership "Work Program" covers these twenty-two areas:

- Air Defense
- Airspace Management
- Consultation, Command, and Control
- Civil Emergency Planning
- Crisis Management
- Democratic Control of Forces and Defense Structures
- Defense Planning, Budgeting, and Resource Management
- National Defense Procurement
- Defense Policy and Strategy
- Military Geography
- Defense Research and Technology
- Global Humanitarian Mine Action
- Language Training
- Consumer Logistics
- Medical Services
- Meteorological Support
- Military Infrastructure
- Political and Defense Efforts against Nuclear, Biological, Chemical (NBC) Proliferation
- Peacekeeping
- Standardization
- Military Exercises and Training
- Military Education, Training, and Doctrine

In addition, the 2000–2002 EAPC "Action Plan" covers these areas through the form of consultations and workshops:

- Political and Security-Related Issues
- Policy Planning
- Arms Control, Disarmament, and Nonproliferation Issues
- Implementation of Arms Control Agreements
- International Terrorism
- Peacekeeping (including knowledge and application of international humanitarian law)
- Defense Economic Issues
- Science (with a related "Science for Peace Program")
- Challenges of Modern Societies (environment)

- Information
- Civil Emergency Planning and Disaster Preparedness (with a Euro-Atlantic Disaster Response Coordination Center [EADRCC] having been established in 1998 at Russian initiative to coordinate with the UN).

The question remains, however, of what should be the ultimate aim of EAPC/PFP. In particular, on December 3, 1993 then Russian Foreign Minister Kozyrev proposed that NACC should evolve from a "NATO+" to a NACC+NATO,WEU,CIS "and all other organizations" as an independent problem-solving body "to avoid feeling a certain paternalism that we experience in the participation in our cooperation," just as then Deputy Russian Foreign Minister Igor Ivanov stated on May 30, 1997, that PFP should be a school for meeting new challenges but not a "prep school" for aspiring NATO members. There has always been a NATO reluctance to cede control over outreach, and surely Russia would, if the NATO consensus decision-making rule was applied to EAPC/PFP, have had reservations about the use of two PFP events in 1998–Exercise Cooperative Assembly in Albania on August 17–22, and Exercise Cooperative Best Effort in Macedonia between September 10–18—to demonstrate NATO support for regional stability and display NATO's capabilities *vis-à-vis* Milosevic (even though an air exercise over the same countries—Exercise Determined Falcon on June 15—with the same purposes was not a PFP event). If the concern is overloading NATO, then an EAPC secretariat should be established with its multinationality reflective of the EAPC.

Looking ahead, Dutch Foreign Minister Hans van Mierlo suggested on December 17, 1997:

Linked to NATO, but also related to the OSCE, the EAPC is an essential part of the European security structure. Both NATO and OSCE have essential roles to play in building a stable and peaceful and undivided Europe, and so has the EAPC.... The comparative advantage of the EAPC over NATO is that the EAPC encompasses almost all OSCE states [all but ten]. The comparative advantage of the EAPC over the OSCE may be that it is better placed for consultation and cooperation on military aspects of security issues, such as peacekeeping. It might very well be that the EAPC will be called upon to prove its worth as a link between OSCE and NATO if the Minsk process [regarding a settlement over Nagorny-Karabakh] would lead to a peace agreement that requires peacekeeping ... in that case we should consider the possibility for the EAPC to play a role in such a peacekeeping operation on the request of the OSCE. The fate of the EAPC is closely linked to the fate of both NATO and the OSCE.[5]

That is, although the difference in number between EAPC and OSCE is only eight countries, and either would pose a challenge for consensus decision making, if the United States and other states do not wish to vest the

OSCE with an operational security role, then perhaps they would be willing to consider EAPC.

Table 6-1
NATO Outreach

EAPC

PFP

NATO-Russia PJC

NATO-Ukraine Commission (NUC)

Mediterranean Dialogue

Southeast Europe Initiative

MEDITERRANEAN DIALOGUE

To placate the oft-voiced but rarely solution-oriented concerns of southern NATO nations, Spain in the lead, facing challenges such as terrorism, uncontrolled migration, and WMD from countries in North Africa, the Middle East, and Southwest Asia, a Mediterranean dialogue was launched on February 8, 1995, at NATO initiative.

Initially, as with NATO diplomatic liaison, the goal was to "explain" NATO to the Southern Mediterranean basin countries and receive their views on general political issues. Yet, only a few days later, then U.S. Deputy Assistant Secretary of Defense Kruzel was already calling for NATO to "go far beyond these initial consultations and commit itself as an institution to developing closer military relations,"[6] as many NATO nations had been doing for decades. No thought was given initially to emulate PFP, even though Egyptian, Jordanian, and Moroccan forces were participating under NATO command in IFOR. The dialogue, carried out on a NATO+partner basis rather than collectively as the EAPC, comprises Mauritania, Morocco, Tunisia, Egypt, Israel, and Jordan (the OSCE adds Algeria but subtracts Mauritania in its Mediterranean Partners for Cooperation group). In both cases, it seems that some are not troubled by merely giving the appearance of focusing on the region without concrete and meaningful follow-up, with WEU having also had a similar experience.

Indeed, for various reasons, the Mediterranean dialogue is not a priority NATO activity. Progress has been slow because: the initiative lacks genuine alliance-wide support, there is no clearly defined threat, the problems of the region seem better suited to the EU and International Financial Institutions (IFIs), NATO outreach is already overextended, there is no consensus within NATO on how to deal with Libya and other "rogue" states, Israel does not afford the same trust to Europe as it does to Washington, Washington does not wish to see the Europeans compete with it in the Middle East peace process, and such contacts alone will not reverse NATO's negative image as a tool of the United States and the former European colonial powers[7] (Malta, ever concerned about the Sixth Fleet, even withdrew from PFP when a socialist government returned to power).

At the same time, the potential risks cannot be dismissed and the search for a partner in the region is surely worth the effort. Indeed, then German Defense Minister Rühe argued that "NATO has obligations going beyond the defense of the territories of its member states and relating to global interest . . . especially the potential for crisis and conflict in the strategic triangle of the Balkans, the Caucasus, and Middle East/North Africa."[8] The 2000 Work Program introduced a substantial number of military activities, even if this will simply replicate part of what individual NATO nations have done for many years. Nevertheless, there is a lobby in NATO in favor of maintaining the dialogue, and NATO is the servant of governments.

SOUTHEAST EUROPE INITIATIVE

At the Washington summit, allies agreed to participate in fostering "nationbuilding" and regional stability in Southeast Europe in the aftermath of the Yugoslav wars. At the summit, allies met with heads of state or foreign ministers from Macedonia, Bulgaria, Romania, Slovenia, and Croatia. It was agreed to pursue consultations based on the EAPC format, but also allowing for a "19+1" format. It can be said that this decision represented a new direction for NATO outreach complementing the security and humanitarian tasks IFOR/SFOR/KFOR conducted. Yugoslavia itself, however, the primary source of tension in the Balkans, is not part of the initiative. Lord Robertson has identified the Southeast Europe Initiative (SEEI) as one of his priorities for NATO, and "we will help aspirant countries from Southeastern Europe to prepare their candidacies for NATO membership"[9]—thus adding another outreach focus not limited to former Warsaw Pact countries.

In addition, there is an EU-proposed Stability Pact for Southeastern Europe that includes a security dimension. Adopted in Cologne on June 10, 1999, the very general, wish-list plan ("to develop a shared strategy for stability and growth of the region") notes NATO's decision to increase cooperation with countries of the region, and that the alliance has "an important role" in achieving the pact's objectives. A specific "working table" has been established on security issues, including combatting organized crime (as NATO has done in Bosnia) and confidence-building measures, with meetings taking place in individual countries or at the OSCE Permanent Council, with the pact having been placed under OSCE "auspices." In addition, NATO nations Greece, Italy, the United States, and Turkey work with Albania, Macedonia, Bulgaria, Romania, and Slovenia in a "Southeast Europe Defense Ministerial" (SEDM) which includes setting up a peacekeeping brigade in the Multinational Peacekeeping Force Southeastern Europe

(MPFSEE) with its HQ in Plovdiv, Bulgaria, an engineering task force, and a "crisis information network." SEEI, SEDM, and the Stability Pact, together with the civilian cross-border Southeast European Cooperation Initiative (SECI), can help pave the way for eventual NATO and EU membership, just as the improvement in Hungarian-Romanian, Polish-German, and Czech-German relations assisted the Madrid three in being invited to join the alliance. Naturally, at some point Serbia-Montenegro should have a role, for its suspension from CSCE in 1992 to the present has had no positive impact on bringing peace and reconstruction to the region, and if NATO can negotiate with the Belgrade regime over a peace settlement and conditions for KFOR, it should not keep it at arms length in the SEEI if all partners agree.

Regrettably, despite all the words about the importance of conflict prevention, it took a disaster to activate this attention, and where the required tens of billions of euros will come from remains to be witnessed—reconstruction funding was logjammed as 1999 came to an end, and the United States insisted that there should be no substantial economic assistance to the country it bombarded until there is a change of regime, certainly testing the proposition that the results of free elections should not be challenged. On December 2 that year, NATO defense ministers approved a "Security Assistance Cooperation Group" to increase the effectiveness of such assistance and promote regional cooperation and transparency on security issues.

It is important for the medium-term not to see the SEEI as a cover for the removal of a NATO presence in the region, just as it is too early to determine when the nations helpful to NATO during IFOR/SFOR/KFOR—Albania, Bulgaria, Macedonia, and Romania—will be rewarded with NATO membership. Nevertheless, as with PFP and enlargement, the NATO intent is to ensure long-term stability by "doing for Southeastern Europe after the conflicts in the former Yugoslavia what we helped to do for Western Europe after World War II."[10]

7

REVISITING THE COMMON
EUROPEAN HOME

Ours is a time for fulfilling the hopes and expectations our peoples
have cherished for decades: steadfast commitment to democracy based
on human rights and fundamental freedoms; prosperity through economic liberty and social justice; and equal security for all countries. . . .
We undertake to build, consolidate and strengthen democracy as the
only system of government of our nations.

Charter of Paris for a New Europe
November 21, 1990

Overcoming the division of Europe does not, of course, automatically require NATO enlargement, for that is only one, however an important
means, of doing so. But because enlargement is open to all OSCE participating states, might NATO eventually become the OSCE, with Russia and
other former Soviet republics as full members? This is not an idle question.
Could such an organization provide both collective defense against external attack and crisis management in nonmember states, as does NATO, and
could it also address tensions and conflicts between its members, which
NATO does not?

Nonetheless, in the interim, what are the prospects for OSCE to provide
security to states who choose to remain outside NATO, whether it be because NATO does not want them, their background is with neutrality, or
they feel no compelling need to join alliances?[1]

It had been a favorite theme for the USSR to equate NATO with the Warsaw Pact, in reality a branch of the Soviet army and which used force only to

suppress its own members, such that one should not exist without the other. Unlike NATO, the Warsaw Treaty stated that it would cease to be effective on the date a "general European Treaty of collective security" came into place, the parties to which would not participate "in any coalition or alliance or conclude any agreement the purposes of which would contradict the purposes of the treaty."[2] The United States responded by noting that NATO grew up "because there is no confidence that all members of the United Nations will observe their covenants," and that the Soviet proposal was but "a maneuver to gain admittance within the wall of the West, to undermine its security."[3] Yet, as late as October 27, 1988, the Warsaw Pact foreign ministers were calling for the "creation of an all-European system of collective security and the simultaneous dissolution of the Warsaw Treaty and NATO."

After the fall of the Berlin Wall, some, including Warsaw Pact countries, thought a new security potential could rest in the inclusive CSCE, later renamed the OSCE in 1995. Some advocates of this course may have only been trying to reassure the USSR as they prepared their path for NATO membership, although early Czechoslovak foreign policy did take on a certain "romantic" tone. For example, both Czechoslovakia and Poland proposed ideas in April 1990 to give the CSCE permanent structures, including a military committee, so as to make CSCE more akin to an organization than an occasional conference. President Vaclav Havel of Czechoslovakia foresaw "in this radically new situation both groupings should gradually move toward the ideal of *an entirely new security system* as a forerunner of the future united Europe, which would provide some sort of security background or security guarantees," and that "NATO, as a more meaningful, more democratic and more effective structure, could with less trouble become the seed of a new European security system than the Warsaw Pact," which, he stated, as it "came into being as the symbol of Stalinist expansion will in time lose all *raison d'être*."[4] This is not dissimilar to Secretary General Wörner's statement cited in the introduction, or to Ambassador Vershbow's reference to NATO as "the nucleus of a cooperative security structure" for all of Europe's democracies.

Yet, because the USSR had long championed CSCE despite disregarding its human rights dimensions, and because this, together with NATO's "new look" and restrictions on German armed forces, was part of the overall understanding to support German unity, NATO proposed on July 6, 1990 the structures adopted at the Paris CSCE summit on November 21 that year: a Council of foreign ministers meeting once a year supported by a small secretariat and specialized branches. Later that year, the NAC declared on December 17–18 that "Security and cooperation in the Europe of tomorrow can best be achieved by a framework of *interlocking institutions* in which the interests of all European states can be accommodated" (emphasis added). This formula, which began with paralysis, rivalry, or duplication of effort (witness the initially separate WEU and NATO Adriatic monitoring operations beginning in 1992, although shortly consolidated as Operation Sharp Guard, and UNPROFOR micromanagement of NATO) to a degree of institutional synergy beginning with IFOR, was explained by a former NATO policy planner as follows:

There was some sympathy for the notion that the Alliance would become the all-encompassing European security organization [as U.S. officials frequently state]. This was, however, a largely marginal view. In fact, there was perhaps more sympathy among members for the idea that the time had probably come for the institution to make a graceful exit. The mainstream view, and the one which ultimately won out, was that the organization, assuming it could successfully transform itself, was still necessary. It would, nevertheless, have to share responsibilities in the European theater whereas for the most part it had previously acted alone [thus the 1992 NATO decisions to consider supporting UNSC-mandated or CSCE-authorized peacekeeping].[5]

As a sign of the changing times, the two confrontational blocs in CSCE of the Warsaw Pact and NATO were replaced by the EU/WEU and the United States/NATO, whereas the traditionally conciliatory neutral and nonaligned group fell apart when the wars in neutral and nonaligned Yugoslavia began. Interestingly, on its own initiative Finland acquired observer status in NACC in 1992, and it was Finland which circumvented French objections to a formal presentation by the NATO Secretary General at the CSCE Helsinki summit that year (even though the presidency of the EU was represented in both his or her national and EU capacities) by having him address a luncheon hosted by the Finnish president (and Finnish protocol made no effort to stop Secretary General Wörner from posing in the "family portrait" of heads of state or government).

Of course, the notion of "interlocking" or "mutually reinforcing" institutions has some way to go. The UN police in Kosovo were still over 3,000 personnel short of what was requested as of January 2000, such that only four out of the twenty-nine municipalities were under the primary responsibility of the UN force, compelling KFOR to take up nonmilitary tasks. There is still the attempt by some to pose a false choice between NATO and the EU as the framework for European security, with there still being no institutional relationship between the two as of the end of 2000. OSCE and the Council of Europe still seem to duplicate each other, whereas it is not clear why both the UN and the OSCE are involved in monitoring in Georgia. And, as discussed, the contribution of the EAPC remains to be seen. Nevertheless, security problems are not solely military, and NATO cannot, and will not, do everything.

Table 7-1
"Mutually Reinforcing" Institutions In Kosovo

KFOR	Peace support
UNHCR	Winterization, mine action coordination
UNMIK	International civilian police, public administration, judicial system
OSCE	Elections, human rights, media, democracy building, Kosovo Police training
EU, World Bank	Reconstruction

Source: Balkans Security: Current and Projected Factors Affecting Regional Stability (Washington, DC: U.S. General Accounting Office, April 2000), p. 80.

Of course, all military tasks regarding the Balkans had been undertaken by the UN, NATO, and the WEU, not the CSCE. Although it had been agreed at the Helsinki summit that CSCE could undertake peacekeeping, it had no dedicated forces or supporting structures, and the participating states agreed that CSCE peacekeeping could not include enforcement action. However, Russia has argued relentlessly that it is the OSCE that should have the key role to play in European security in the construction of what it still believes will be a multipolar world, with Russia as one of the indispensable poles. Russia has repeatedly called for the OSCE to play a "coordinating" role or serve as the "aegis" for other organizations in a new security system in which NATO could play a part but only as a "political-peacekeeping" organization and not as a military alliance.

Table 7-2
European Security "Architecture"

CRISIS → NATO-led, EU/WEU-led w-w/o NATO, nations,
NATO Partners w-w/o UNSC mandate or OSCE authority,
OSCE-led → **RESPONSE** →
NATO, UN, EU/WEU, OSCE, IFIs, NGOs, nations → **RECONSTRUCTION**

However, because of *inter alia* competition among organizations most vividly demonstrated in the WEU-NATO and OSCE-Council of Europe contexts and a reluctance by some to assign legitimacy to the amorphous "CIS," a generalized feeling still exists that OSCE is too unwieldy to accomplish more than limited preventive diplomacy and democracy building within its means. Moreover, the promoter since 1994 of the idea of a "Security Model" for the 21st century, Russia has never been able to answer very pertinent questions, such that "The level of contradiction and emotion was so high that even the work programme for the negotiating body—the so-called Security Model Committee—was sometimes a contentious one. . . . [T]he Russians constantly complained about NATO enlargement."[6]

For example, Russia's 1997 National Security "Blueprint" states: The creation of a model for ensuring global, regional and subregional security geared to the 21st century and based on the principles of equality and indivisible security for all must become an absolute condition for the implementation of Russia's foreign policy efforts. This presupposes the creation of a fundamentally new system of European-Atlantic security in which the OSCE will play a coordinating role.[7]

And yet

- OSCE has never undertaken peacekeeping, in part because of a perceived Russian aversion to attach any organization except the "CIS" to conduct operations on the territory of the former USSR, and a Western preference for NATO or the EU. Russia proposed a permanent OSCE peacekeeping HQ and stand-by forces, but supported multinational operations only where "both possible and advisable." Nevertheless, by enhancing OSCE's profile, legitimacy could be given to Russia or the CIS as an agent of the OSCE, and Russian forces perform the overwhelming bulk of peacekeeping, together with a degree of bullying to maintain basing rights, in Georgia and Tadjikistan, and have delayed withdrawing from Moldova until a settlement of the status of the Transdniestr is reached, although this is explained normally as a problem of costs.
- In 1997, Russia proposed OSCE security guarantees whereby states would assist another facing aggression as defined by the UNSC. But it never elaborated what they would mean in practice, and opposes changing the consensus rule of decision making (meaning that an aggressor could veto his punishers). Likewise, in his September 1997 letter to Western leaders, President Yeltsin suggested joint NATO and Russian guarantees to Central Europe as an alternative to NATO enlargement. Ukraine has also proposed OSCE guarantees to neutral states from European and Euro-Atlantic organizations (read NATO).
- Although echoing Gaullist theology, President Yeltsin's pronouncements that European security should be a matter for Europeans themselves, Russia included, are hardly helpful from a transatlantic perspective.
- Why would any NATO member or aspiring ally wish to abandon the benefits of having its national security supported collectively in favor of belonging to a purely "political/peacekeeping" organization? And how would such a hypothetical transformation be measured: how different is a robust peace support force from one able to defend territory? Moreover, the armed forces belong not to NATO, but to the individual members.

- Since the adoption of the 1975 CSCE Helsinki Final Act, human rights have been viewed as a matter of legitimate concern for any participating state and not exclusively an internal question, a principle which expanded to cover *all* OSCE norms and commitments. The 1994 Code of Conduct on Politico-Military Aspects of Security reiterated the principle that armed forces must use proportional force in internal conflicts. Yet, on November 18, 1999, at the Istanbul OSCE summit, President Yeltsin stated: "You have no right to criticize Russia for Chechnya," and, with reference to Allied Force, that there was no justification for "the appeals for humanitarian interference—this is a new idea—in the internal affairs of another state, even when this is done on the pretext of protecting human rights and freedom." Instead, he stated, "it is more urgently necessary than ever before that our principal commandment for our joint efforts in Europe should be, 'Avoid doing harm.' "[8] Thus, the December 14–16, 1999 visit to Chechnya of the OSCE Chairman-in-Office (CiO), Norwegian Foreign Minister Knut Vollebæk, who called without any more success than NATO, the Council of Europe, the EU, or the G-7 for a ceasefire in Chechnya, was described as having "an air of unreality": Vollebæk stated that Russia "does not need the international community to assist them,"[9] even though it would be in Russia's interests to resort to the OSCE if only as a fig leaf to counter "NATO-centrism." A European official conceded that the visit of the CiO was simply "a sop to their [Russia's] need and our need to show that something happened,"[10] the fact that there were no results notwithstanding. Consequently, one must question whether OSCE can be too easily manipulated for propaganda purposes. In any event, Foreign Minister Igor Ivanov's remark that "Human rights are no reason to interfere in the internal affairs of a state"[11] can only be considered regrettable and unacceptable in light of the fact that it was in Moscow in 1991 that the CSCE adopted the principle that violations of human rights were matters of "direct and legitimate concern" to all participating states, and where a "mechanism" was agreed that would allow six states to initiate fact-finding missions without the consent of the suspected violating state.

In light of the above, it would not be unreasonable to conclude that the Russian grand, if intangible, schemes for OSCE, including the notion that it should "coordinate" the work of other organizations and be put on a legal footing, seem more about preventing something—West Germany in NATO in the 1950s, a united Germany in NATO in 1990, and NATO enlargement in the 1990s and thereafter, and preventing too intrusive a role for OSCE in Russia and its areas of interest—than as offering a sensible security alternative for Europe. Thus, if Russia is indeed trying to distance itself from the West, then arguments that PFP and the PJC are "ill-suited to enhancing security arrangements" in the former Soviet space compared to OSCE are not self-evident.[12]

As a result, the last OSCE summit of the 20th century, in Istanbul in November 1999, largely took stock of events rather than providing a watershed comparable to prior landmarks such as the 1975 Helsinki Final Act, the 1990 Charter of Paris, and the 1992 Helsinki summit. The closest passage in the 1999 so-called "Charter for European Security" (the result of the Russia-proposed Security Model exercise) which comes close to suggesting a security guarantee is rather a jumble:

> We will consult promptly . . . with a participating State seeking assistance in realizing its right to individual or collective self-defense in the event that its sovereignty, territorial integrity and political independence are threatened . . . [and] we will consider jointly the nature of the threat and actions that may be required in defense of our common values.

But defending values and assisting a state in defense of its sovereignty, territorial integrity, or political independence are not the same thing. It is not clear to what participating states committed themselves, and a previous placeholder for resort to "military action" was dropped because of the strong preference in the EU, Washington, and Moscow for strictly "cooperative security" and the consensus rule of decision making. There is, thus, no OSCE *Sturmbandmacht* for peace support, although there is nothing preventing participating states to establish such a force, which could naturally draw on NATO. OSCE police, which began work in 1998 in Croatia, cannot even engage in law enforcement, as was proposed for Istanbul (subsequently the European Council agreed in June 2000 at Maria da Feira, Portugal, to create a 5,000-strong force by 2003 to include executive policing). Here, it might also be useful to consider convening regular meetings of the Interior Ministers and Chiefs of Defense Staff (CHODs), which would fulfill the idea of OSCE military representative meetings envisaged by Czechoslovakia in 1990, to at least explore options.

Small wonder, then, that the OSCE Charter is so inept to the needs of the times. The State Department pushed the spin envelope to yet another embarrassing degree by declaring as "an important step" the sentence in the charter reading "threats to our security can stem from conflicts within states as well as from conflicts between states"—as if this was some revelation, as if CSCE/OSCE had not always concerned itself with internal domestic affairs, and as if the charter itself did not preface that sentence with the affirmation that such risks "become more obvious." What was missing was the relevant statement by NATO Secretary General Solana a year before on January 28, 1999: "What we have seen in Yugoslavia during the past decade is that it is very difficult to stop internal conflicts if the international community is not willing to use force."[13] Although the 1994 Code of Conduct states that the participating states will base their mutual security relations upon "a cooperative approach," the OSCE stands for Organization for Security *and* Cooperation in Europe, not Security exclusively *through* Cooperation. This fact is manifested by the ability of only some states to call up fact-finding missions in another state without the latter's consent, and by the consensus-minus-one rule.

This is not to suggest that the OSCE, with a small permanent secretariat of less than 300 individuals (the 1,100 international staff in the field are seconded and paid by their national government), a purely administrative and thus largely invisible secretary general, a budget which amounted in 2000 to a mere $200 million (cf. NATO's common budget of $1.5 billion), and which is compelled to seek continuously emergency funding, does not play an important role in its 20 missions and other field activities. It is not the fault of the organization that the mandates the participating states assign to it demand the seemingly impossible, to wit:

- The Assistance Group to Chechnya, established in 1995 with six individuals, could hardly be expected to "promote respect for human rights" or "promote the peaceful resolution of the crisis," and was withdrawn from Grozny two years later pending an improvement in the security situation (it was agreed that it would return in 2000, with two staff members); Russia delayed in allowing an OSCE presence in neighboring Ingushetia, where hundreds of thousands of people displaced by the fighting have fled.

- The eight–member mission to Georgia, established in 1993, has proved unable to facilitate a "lasting political settlement."

- The 2,000–staff KVM backed up by NATO overflight operation Eagle Eye had to be withdrawn because of the security environment (although this may have been a preplanned event to demonstrate that there was no alternative to the NATO air campaign,[14] or as an adjunct to prebombing intelligence gathering on Serbian positions, as some KVM members have suggested.

- The internationally discredited Belarusian National Assembly completely bypassed the suggestions of the OSCE Advisory and Monitoring Group by imposing an undemocratic electoral law in January 2000, and the tasking to the OSCE Mission in Kosovo to bring about "mutual respect and reconciliation" would seem to be mission impossible.

- It was the Contact Group that played the key political role in Bosnia and then Kosovo, despite its "ineffectiveness" in Ambassador Holbrooke's view,[15] yet there is no formal OSCE Security Council–type structure, and OSCE was not given a larger role in Kosovo despite UK and U.S. preferences for OSCE over the UN.

- OSCE still has no international legal status, despite the 1995 change in name.

- The FRY's suspension to vent cost free condemnation since 1992 from OSCE appears to have contributed nothing positive, and led to the expulsion the following year with impunity of the three preventive diplomacy "missions of long duration" in Kosovo, Sandjak, and Vojvodina. The absence of OSCE from Yugoslavia, save for Kosovo, in 2000 also hardly helped clarify the ambiguous results of the October presidential elections, even though the monitoring of votes has become a primary OSCE task, and certainly no other election in Europe had more significance in the Balkans. Milosevic conceded defeat on October 6, 2000 in the presidential elections, and OSCE may be called upon to play yet another democracy- building role in the Balkans.

Despite these obstacles and unmet expectations, however, OSCE still remains the primary laboratory for the new Europe, exploring security in its "comprehensive" sense, including social and economic questions. Its human rights reporting can provide needed light in confused situations such as in the Balkans and Chechnya. It is the quintessential "conscience of the continent." But because of the refusal among the OSCE participating states locked into the mantra of "cooperative security" to include enforcement and marry diplomacy with force, and to adapt accordingly the consensus decision making rule which has been described as "a major disadvantage which prevents the OSCE from having a mechanism of adopting and implementing decisions,"[16] NATO will remain at the center of European security, working with, but not being submerged by, the OSCE. The notion of the EAPC serving as the security arm of OSCE could perhaps strike a balance such that Russia and all other EAPC members feel they have the sense of shaping decisions on the operational side of conflict prevention and management in support of OSCE decisions and commitments. It would be an important test of the future of OSCE, and of Russia's intentions, if the principle of humanitarian intervention, as discussed in Chapter 3, might find expression in the Charter for European Security, with EAPC perhaps serving as one of the operational fora for implementation should new thinking come about.

Otherwise, the fact that the OSCE, while routinely urging respect for human and national minority rights and rejecting ethnic cleansing and mass expulsion, could not have acted as NATO acted in Kosovo is hardly an endorsement of a document purporting to call itself a charter for European Security—"have we eaten on the insane root that takes reason prisoner?" (Macbeth, I: 3). If the security of the individual is to have meaning on a Euro-Atlantic scale, then participating States must seriously address how to implement the Charter's pledge in paragraph 14 to explore ways to increase OSCE effectiveness "to deal with cases of clear, gross, and continuing violations" of its principles and commitments.

Breaking the levee to constructing credible "comprehensive security" must demand priority. "It is simplicity itself," as Mr. Sherlock Holmes put it in "A Scandal in Bohemia."

CONCLUSION

> The ultimate political purpose of the Alliance is to achieve a just and
> lasting peaceful order in Europe accompanied by appropriate security
> guarantees.
>
> *The Future Tasks of the Alliance* (Harmel Report)
> North Atlantic Council
> December 14, 1967

In 1957, four years after Stalin's demise, a "Wise Men" report to the NAC
asked: "Can a loose association of sovereign states hold together at all without the common binding fear of force?" The answer was affirmative:

> [T]he long term aim of NATO was the development of an Atlantic Community
> whose roots are deeper than the necessity for common defense . . . NATO must be-
> come more than a military alliance. . . . This implies nothing less than the permanent
> association of the free Atlantic peoples for the promotion of their greater unity and
> the protection and the advancement of the interests which, as free democracies,
> they have in common.

Although providing for the common defense remains NATO's *raison
d'être*, the Wise Men's words are as relevant today and for the future as they
were then. They remain NATO's essential job description. Only NATO, under sustained U.S. leadership, can provide the core of democratic security
in Europe by sustaining the vital transatlantic bridge between the United
States and Europe. Only the alliance can balance a still unpredictable Rus-

sia while seeking to draw it closer into the Western mainstream. NATO can prove indispensable in responding to the kinds of challenges the wars in former Yugoslavia dramatically demonstrated. And it is NATO together with the EU which are the unchallenged magnet of attraction for the new and emerging democracies, whose embedding in the West offers the best hope for peace and prosperity.

The "new NATO," to be sure, remains a work in progress. The alliance and its relationship to other institutions confronts no shortage of issues, as this volume endeavored to explain. To review:

- If the UN Charter were up for review, how might it differ from the original text?

- How is OSCE contributing to the ultimate objective, as stated in the 1999 Charter for European Security, of "the formation of a common and indivisible security space"? Why can the 189 members of the UN continue to vest confidence in the fifteen-member (possibly to be expanded) Security Council to take decisions about peace enforcement, but decline to do so in the regional Euro-Atlantic/Eurasian context?

- Has the legal basis of Operation Allied Force been sufficiently examined? Does an independent jus cogens of humanitarian intervention exist in international law?

- Is NATO enlargement in whole or in part a hedge against Russia? Is this not simply balance of power at work, and does it set natural limits to the NATO-Russia partnership?

- What will be the security and defense dimension of the EU?

- How does a state undertake force planning in the absence of a compelling threat? Are the NATO nations sufficiently attuned to the need to review command and force structures?

- What is the future of neutrality?

- Can future zones of big power conflicts be foreseen? Could NATO play a stabilizing role in the former USSR?

- How are nuclear deterrence and missile defenses to be shaped amidst a changing environment of proliferators?

- What is the ultimate purpose of the EAPC?

But there is no alternative to ensuring that the Atlantic Alliance remains the primary contractor in the effort to shape a stable security order in Europe grounded in partnership, democratic values, and solidarity. And discharging that fundamental task will, as always, have to flow from Washington, DC.

Appendix A

NATO PRESS RELEASE: THE ALLIANCE'S STRATEGIC CONCEPT

**Approved by the Heads of State and Government participating
in the meeting of the North Atlantic Council in Washington
D.C. on 23rd and 24th April 1999**

INTRODUCTION

1. At their Summit meeting in Washington in April 1999, NATO Heads of State and Government approved the Alliance's new Strategic Concept.

2. NATO has successfully ensured the freedom of its members and prevented war in Europe during the 40 years of the Cold War. By combining defence with dialogue, it played an indispensable role in bringing East-West confrontation to a peaceful end. The dramatic changes in the Euro-Atlantic strategic landscape brought by the end of the Cold War were reflected in the Alliance's 1991 Strategic Concept. There have, however, been further profound political and security developments since then.

3. The dangers of the Cold War have given way to more promising, but also challenging prospects, to new opportunities and risks. A new Europe of greater integration is emerging, and a Euro-Atlantic security structure is evolving in which NATO plays a central part. The Alliance has been at the heart of efforts to establish new patterns of cooperation and mutual understanding across the Euro-Atlantic region and has committed itself to essential new activities in the interest of a wider stability. It has shown the depth of that commitment in its efforts to put an end to the immense human suffering created by conflict in the Balkans. The years since the end of the Cold

War have also witnessed important developments in arms control, a process to which the Alliance is fully committed. The Alliance's role in these positive developments has been underpinned by the comprehensive adaptation of its approach to security and of its procedures and structures. The last ten years have also seen, however, the appearance of complex new risks to Euro-Atlantic peace and stability, including oppression, ethnic conflict, economic distress, the collapse of political order, and the proliferation of weapons of mass destruction.

4. The Alliance has an indispensable role to play in consolidating and preserving the positive changes of the recent past, and in meeting current and future security challenges. It has, therefore, a demanding agenda. It must safeguard common security interests in an environment of further, often unpredictable change. It must maintain collective defence and reinforce the transatlantic link and ensure a balance that allows the European Allies to assume greater responsibility. It must deepen its relations with its partners and prepare for the accession of new members. It must, above all, maintain the political will and the military means required by the entire range of its missions.

5. This new Strategic Concept will guide the Alliance as it pursues this agenda. It expresses NATO's enduring purpose and nature and its fundamental security tasks, identifies the central features of the new security environment, specifies the elements of the Alliance's broad approach to security, and provides guidelines for the further adaptation of its military forces.

PART I: THE PURPOSE AND TASKS OF THE ALLIANCE

6. NATO's essential and enduring purpose, set out in the Washington Treaty, is to safeguard the freedom and security of all its members by political and military means. Based on common values of democracy, human rights and the rule of law, the Alliance has striven since its inception to secure a just and lasting peaceful order in Europe. It will continue to do so. The achievement of this aim can be put at risk by crisis and conflict affecting the security of the Euro-Atlantic area. The Alliance therefore not only ensures the defence of its members but contributes to peace and stability in this region.

7. The Alliance embodies the transatlantic link by which the security of North America is permanently tied to the security of Europe. It is the practical expression of effective collective effort among its members in support of their common interests.

8. The fundamental guiding principle by which the Alliance works is that of common commitment and mutual co-operation among sovereign states in support of the indivisibility of security for all of its members. Solidarity and cohesion within the Alliance, through daily cooperation in both

the political and military spheres, ensure that no single Ally is forced to rely upon its own national efforts alone in dealing with basic security challenges. Without depriving member states of their right and duty to assume their sovereign responsibilities in the field of defence, the Alliance enables them through collective effort to realise their essential national security objectives.

9. The resulting sense of equal security among the members of the Alliance, regardless of differences in their circumstances or in their national military capabilities, contributes to stability in the Euro-Atlantic area. The Alliance does not seek these benefits for its members alone, but is committed to the creation of conditions conducive to increased partnership, cooperation, and dialogue with others who share its broad political objectives.

10. To achieve its essential purpose, as an Alliance of nations committed to the Washington Treaty and the United Nations Charter, the Alliance performs the following fundamental security tasks:

Security: To provide one of the indispensable foundations for a stable Euro-Atlantic security environment, based on the growth of democratic institutions and commitment to the peaceful resolution of disputes, in which no country would be able to intimidate or coerce any other through the threat or use of force.

Consultation: To serve, as provided for in Article 4 of the Washington Treaty, as an essential transatlantic forum for Allied consultations on any issues that affect their vital interests, including possible developments posing risks for members' security, and for appropriate co-ordination of their efforts in fields of common concern.

Deterrence and Defence: To deter and defend against any threat of aggression against any NATO member state as provided for in Articles 5 and 6 of the Washington Treaty.

And in order to enhance the security and stability of the Euro-Atlantic area:

- Crisis Management: To stand ready, case-by-case and by consensus, in conformity with Article 7 of the Washington Treaty, to contribute to effective conflict prevention and to engage actively in crisis management, including crisis response operations.
- Partnership: To promote wide-ranging partnership, cooperation, and dialogue with other countries in the Euro-Atlantic area, with the aim of increasing transparency, mutual confidence and the capacity for joint action with the Alliance.

11. In fulfilling its purpose and fundamental security tasks, the Alliance will continue to respect the legitimate security interests of others, and seek

the peaceful resolution of disputes as set out in the Charter of the United Nations. The Alliance will promote peaceful and friendly international relations and support democratic institutions. The Alliance does not consider itself to be any country's adversary.

PART II: STRATEGIC PERSPECTIVES

The Evolving Strategic Environment

12. The Alliance operates in an environment of continuing change. Developments in recent years have been generally positive, but uncertainties and risks remain which can develop into acute crises. Within this evolving context, NATO has played an essential part in strengthening Euro-Atlantic security since the end of the Cold War. Its growing political role; its increased political and military partnership, cooperation and dialogue with other states, including with Russia, Ukraine and Mediterranean Dialogue countries; its continuing openness to the accession of new members; its collaboration with other international organisations; its commitment, exemplified in the Balkans, to conflict prevention and crisis management, including through peace support operations: all reflect its determination to shape its security environment and enhance the peace and stability of the Euro-Atlantic area.

13. In parallel, NATO has successfully adapted to enhance its ability to contribute to Euro-Atlantic peace and stability. Internal reform has included a new command structure, including the Combined Joint Task Force (CJTF) concept, the creation of arrangements to permit the rapid deployment of forces for the full range of the Alliance's missions, and the building of the European Security and Defence Identity (ESDI) within the Alliance.

14. The United Nations (UN), the Organisation for Security and Cooperation in Europe (OSCE), the European Union (EU), and the Western European Union (WEU) have made distinctive contributions to Euro-Atlantic security and stability. Mutually reinforcing organisations have become a central feature of the security environment.

15. The United Nations Security Council has the primary responsibility for the maintenance of international peace and security and, as such, plays a crucial role in contributing to security and stability in the Euro-Atlantic area.

16. The OSCE, as a regional arrangement, is the most inclusive security organisation in Europe, which also includes Canada and the United States, and plays an essential role in promoting peace and stability, enhancing cooperative security, and advancing democracy and human rights in Europe. The OSCE is particularly active in the fields of preventive diplomacy, conflict prevention, crisis management, and post-conflict rehabilitation. NATO and the OSCE have developed close practical cooperation, espe-

cially with regard to the international effort to bring peace to the former Yugoslavia.

17. The European Union has taken important decisions and given a further impetus to its efforts to strengthen its security and defence dimension. This process will have implications for the entire Alliance, and all European Allies should be involved in it, building on arrangements developed by NATO and the WEU. The development of a common foreign and security policy (CFSP) includes the progressive framing of a common defence policy. Such a policy, as called for in the Amsterdam Treaty, would be compatible with the common security and defence policy established within the framework of the Washington Treaty. Important steps taken in this context include the incorporation of the WEU's Petersberg tasks into the Treaty on European Union and the development of closer institutional relations with the WEU.

18. As stated in the 1994 Summit declaration and reaffirmed in Berlin in 1996, the Alliance fully supports the development of the European Security and Defence Identity within the Alliance by making available its assets and capabilities for WEU-led operations. To this end, the Alliance and the WEU have developed a close relationship and put into place key elements of the ESDI as agreed in Berlin. In order to enhance peace and stability in Europe and more widely, the European Allies are strengthening their capacity for action, including by increasing their military capabilities. The increase of the responsibilities and capacities of the European Allies with respect to security and defence enhances the security environment of the Alliance.

19. The stability, transparency, predictability, lower levels of armaments, and verification which can be provided by arms control and non-proliferation agreements support NATO's political and military efforts to achieve its strategic objectives. The Allies have played a major part in the significant achievements in this field. These include the enhanced stability produced by the CFE Treaty, the deep reductions in nuclear weapons provided for in the START treaties; the signature of the Comprehensive Test Ban Treaty, the indefinite and unconditional extension of the Nuciear Non-Proliferation Treaty, the accession to it of Belarus, Kazakhstan, and Ukraine as non-nuclear weapons states, and the entry into force of the Chemical Weapons Convention. The Ottawa Convention to ban anti-personnel landmines and similar agreements make an important contribution to alleviating human suffering. There are welcome prospects for further advances in arms control in conventional weapons and with respect to nuclear, chemical, and biological (NBC) weapons.

Security challenges and risks

20. Notwithstanding positive developments in the strategic environment and the fact that large-scale conventional aggression against the Alli-

ance is highly unlikely, the possibility of such a threat emerging over the longer term exists. The security of the Alliance remains subject to a wide variety of military and non-military risks which are multi-directional and often difficult to predict. These risks include uncertainty and instability in and around the Euro-Atlantic area and the possibility of regional crises at the periphery of the Alliance, which could evolve rapidly. Some countries in and around the Euro-Atlantic area face serious economic, social and political difficulties. Ethnic and religious rivalries, territorial disputes, inadequate or failed efforts at reform, the abuse of human rights, and the dissolution of states can lead to local and even regional instability. The resulting tensions could lead to crises affecting Euro-Atlantic stability, to human suffering, and to armed conflicts. Such conflicts could affect the security of the Alliance by spilling over into neighbouring countries, including NATO countries, or in other ways, and could also affect the security of other states.

21. The existence of powerful nuclear forces outside the Alliance also constitutes a significant factor which the Alliance has to take into account if security and stability in the Euro-Atlantic area are to be maintained.

22. The proliferation of NBC weapons and their means of delivery remains a matter of serious concern. In spite of welcome progress in strengthening international non-proliferation regimes, major challenges with respect to proliferation remain. The Alliance recognises that proliferation can occur despite efforts to prevent it and can pose a direct military threat to the Allies' populations, territory, and forces. Some states, including on NATO's periphery and in other regions, sell or acquire or try to acquire NBC weapons and delivery means. Commodities and technology that could be used to build these weapons of mass destruction and their delivery means are becoming more common, while detection and prevention of illicit trade in these materials and know-how continues to be difficult. Non-state actors have shown the potential to create and use some of these weapons.

23. The global spread of technology that can be of use in the production of weapons may result in the greater availability of sophisticated military capabilities, permitting adversaries to acquire highly capable offensive and defensive air, land, and sea-borne systems, cruise missiles, and other advanced weaponry. In addition, state and non-state adversaries may try to exploit the Alliance's growing reliance on information systems through information operations designed to disrupt such systems. They may attempt to use strategies of this kind to counter NATO's superiority in traditional weaponry.

24. Any armed attack on the territory of the Allies, from whatever direction, would be covered by Articles 5 and 6 of the Washington Treaty. However, Alliance security must also take account of the global context. Alliance security interests can be affected by other risks of a wider nature, including

acts of terrorism, sabotage and organised crime, and by the disruption of the flow of vital resources. The uncontrolled movement of large numbers of people, particularly as a consequence of armed conflicts, can also pose problems for security and stability affecting the Alliance. Arrangements exist within the Alliance for consultation among the Allies under Article 4 of the Washington Treaty and, where appropriate, co-ordination of their efforts including their responses to risks of this kind.

PART III: THE APPROACH TO SECURITY IN THE 21ST CENTURY

25. The Alliance is committed to a broad approach to security, which recognises the importance of political, economic, social and environmental factors in addition to the indispensable defence dimension. This broad approach forms the basis for the Alliance to accomplish its fundamental security tasks effectively, and its increasing effort to develop effective cooperation with other European and Euro-Atlantic organisations as well as the United Nations. Our collective aim is to build a European security architecture in which the Alliance's contribution to the security and stability of the Euro-Atlantic area and the contribution of these other international organisations are complementary and mutually reinforcing, both in deepening relations among Euro-Atlantic countries and in managing crises. NATO remains the essential forum for consultation among the Allies and the forum for agreement on policies bearing on the security and defence commitments of its members under the Washington Treaty.

26. The Alliance seeks to preserve peace and to reinforce Euro-Atlantic security and stability by: the preservation of the transatlantic link; the maintenance of effective military capabilities sufficient for deterrence and defence and to fulfil the full range of its missions; the development of the European Security and Defence Identity within the Alliance; an overall capability to manage crises successfully; its continued openness to new members; and the continued pursuit of partnership, cooperation, and dialogue with other nations as part of its co-operative approach to Euro-Atlantic security, including in the field of arms control and disarmament.

The Transatlantic Link

27. NATO is committed to a strong and dynamic partnership between Europe and North America in support of the values and interests they share. The security of Europe and that of North America are indivisible. Thus the Alliance's commitment to the indispensable transatlantic link and the collective defence of its members is fundamental to its credibility and to the security and stability of the Euro-Atlantic area.

The Maintenance Of Alliance Military Capabilities

28. The maintenance of an adequate military capability and clear preparedness to act collectively in the common defence remain central to the Alliance's security objectives. Such a capability, together with political solidarity, remains at the core of the Alliance's ability to prevent any attempt at coercion or intimidation, and to guarantee that military aggression directed against the Alliance can never be perceived as an option with any prospect of success.

29. Military capabilities effective under the full range of foreseeable circumstances are also the basis of the Alliance's ability to contribute to conflict prevention and crisis management through non-Article 5 crisis response operations. These missions can be highly demanding and can place a premium on the same political and military qualities, such as cohesion, multinational training, and extensive prior planning, that would be essential in an Article 5 situation. Accordingly, while they may pose special requirements, they will be handled through a common set of Alliance structures and procedures.

The European Security And Defence Identity

30. The Alliance, which is the foundation of the collective defence of its members and through which common security objectives will be pursued wherever possible, remains committed to a balanced and dynamic transatlantic partnership. The European Allies have taken decisions to enable them to assume greater responsibilities in the security and defence field in order to enhance the peace and stability of the Euro-Atlantic area and thus the security of all Allies. On the basis of decisions taken by the Alliance, in Berlin in 1996 and subsequently, the European Security and Defence Identity will continue to be developed within NATO. This process will require close cooperation between NATO, the WEU and, if and when appropriate, the European Union. It will enable all European Allies to make a more coherent and effective contribution to the missions and activities of the Alliance as an expression of our shared responsibilities; it will reinforce the transatlantic partnership; and it will assist the European Allies to act by themselves as required through the readiness of the Alliance, on a case-by-case basis and by consensus, to make its assets and capabilities available for operations in which the Alliance is not engaged militarily under the political control and strategic direction either of the WEU or as otherwise agreed, taking into account the full participation of all European Allies if they were so to choose.

Conflict Prevention And Crisis Management

31. In pursuit of its policy of preserving peace, preventing war, and enhancing security and stability and as set out in the fundamental security

tasks, NATO will seek, in cooperation with other organisations, to prevent conflict, or, should a crisis arise, to contribute to its effective management, consistent with international law, including through the possibility of conducting non-Article 5 crisis response operations. The Alliance's preparedness to carry out such operations supports the broader objective of reinforcing and extending stability and often involves the participation of NATO's Partners. NATO recalls its offer, made in Brussels in 1994, to support on a case-by-case basis in accordance with its own procedures, peacekeeping and other operations under the authority of the UN Security Council or the responsibility of the OSCE, including by making available Alliance resources and expertise. In this context NATO recalls its subsequent decisions with respect to crisis response operations in the Balkans. Taking into account the necessity for Alliance solidarity and cohesion, participation in any such operation or mission will remain subject to decisions of member states in accordance with national constitutions.

32. NATO will make full use of partnership, cooperation and dialogue and its links to other organisations to contribute to preventing crises and, should they arise, defusing them at an early stage. A coherent approach to crisis management, as in any use of force by the Alliance, will require the Alliance's political authorities to choose and co-ordinate appropriate responses from a range of both political and military measures and to exercise close political control at all stages.

Partnership, Cooperation, And Dialogue

33. Through its active pursuit of partnership, cooperation, and dialogue, the Alliance is a positive force in promoting security and stability throughout the Euro-Atlantic area. Through outreach and openness, the Alliance seeks to preserve peace, support and promote democracy, contribute to prosperity and progress, and foster genuine partnership with and among all democratic Euro-Atlantic countries. This aims at enhancing the security of all, excludes nobody, and helps to overcome divisions and disagreements that could lead to instability and conflict.

34. The Euro-Atlantic Partnership Council (EAPC) will remain the overarching framework for all aspects of NATO's cooperation with its Partners. It offers an expanded political dimension for both consultation and cooperation. EAPC consultations build increased transparency and confidence among its members on security issues, contribute to conflict prevention and crisis management, and develop practical cooperation activities, including in civil emergency planning, and scientific and environmental affairs.

35. The Partnership for Peace is the principal mechanism for forging practical security links between the Alliance and its Partners and for enhancing interoperability between Partners and NATO. Through detailed

programmes that reflect individual Partners' capacities and interests, Allies and Partners work towards transparency in national defence planning and budgeting; democratic control of defence forces; preparedness for civil disasters and other emergencies; and the development of the ability to work together, including in NATO-led PfP operations. The Alliance is committed to increasing the role the Partners play in PfP decision-making and planning, and making PfP more operational. NATO has undertaken to consult with any active participant in the Partnership if that Partner perceives a direct threat to its territorial integrity, political independence, or security.

36. Russia plays a unique role in Euro-Atlantic security. Within the framework of the NATO-Russia Founding Act on Mutual Relations, Cooperation and Security, NATO and Russia have committed themselves to developing their relations on the basis of common interest, reciprocity and transparency to achieve a lasting and inclusive peace in the Euro-Atlantic area based on the principles of democracy and co-operative security. NATO and Russia have agreed to give concrete substance to their shared commitment to build a stable, peaceful and undivided Europe. A strong, stable and enduring partnership between NATO and Russia is essential to achieve lasting stability in the Euro-Atlantic area.

37. Ukraine occupies a special place in the Euro-Atlantic security environment and is an important and valuable partner in promoting stability and common democratic values. NATO is committed to further strengthening its distinctive partnership with Ukraine on the basis of the NATO-Ukraine Charter, including political consultations on issues of common concern and a broad range of practical cooperation activities. The Alliance continues to support Ukrainian sovereignty and independence, territorial integrity, democratic development, economic prosperity and its status as a non-nuclear weapons state as key factors of stability and security in central and eastern Europe and in Europe as a whole.

38. The Mediterranean is an area of special interest to the Alliance. Security in Europe is closely linked to security and stability in the Mediterranean. NATO's Mediterranean Dialogue process is an integral part of NATO's co-operative approach to security. It provides a framework for confidence building, promotes transparency and cooperation in the region, and reinforces and is reinforced by other international efforts. The Alliance is committed to developing progressively the political, civil, and military aspects of the Dialogue with the aim of achieving closer cooperation with, and more active involvement by, countries that are partners in this Dialogue.

Enlargement

39. The Alliance remains open to new members under Article 10 of the Washington Treaty. It expects to extend further invitations in coming years

to nations willing and able to assume the responsibilities and obligations of membership, and as NATO determines that the inclusion of these nations would serve the overall political and strategic interests of the Alliance, strengthen its effectiveness and cohesion, and enhance overall European security and stability. To this end, NATO has established a programme of activities to assist aspiring countries in their preparations for possible future membership in the context of its wider relationship with them. No European democratic country whose admission would fulfil the objectives of the Treaty will be excluded from consideration.

Arms Control, Disarmament, And Non-Proliferation

40. The Alliance's policy of support for arms control, disarmament, and non-proliferation will continue to play a major role in the achievement of the Alliance's security objectives. The Allies seek to enhance security and stability at the lowest possible level of forces consistent with the Alliance's ability to provide for collective defence and to fulfil the full range of its missions. The Alliance will continue to ensure that—as an important part of its broad approach to security—defence and arms control, disarmament, and non-proliferation objectives remain in harmony. The Alliance will continue to actively contribute to the development of arms control, disarmament, and non-proliferation agreements as well as to confidence and security building measures. The Allies take seriously their distinctive role in promoting a broader, more comprehensive and more verifiable international arms control and disarmament process. The Alliance will enhance its political efforts to reduce dangers arising from the proliferation of weapons of mass destruction and their means of delivery. The principal non-proliferation goal of the Alliance and its members is to prevent proliferation from occurring or, should it occur, to reverse it through diplomatic means. The Alliance attaches great importance to the continuing validity and the full implementation by all parties of the CFE Treaty as an essential element in ensuring the stability of the Euro-Atlantic area.

PART IV: GUIDELINES FOR THE ALLIANCE'S FORCES

Principles Of Alliance Strategy

41. The Alliance will maintain the necessary military capabilities to accomplish the full range of NATO's missions. The principles of Allied solidarity and strategic unity remain paramount for all Alliance missions. Alliance forces must safeguard NATO's military effectiveness and freedom of action. The security of all Allies is indivisible: an attack on one is an attack on all. With respect to collective defence under Article 5 of the Washington Treaty, the combined military forces of the Alliance must be capable of deterring any potential aggression against it, of stopping an aggressor's ad-

vance as far forward as possible should an attack nevertheless occur, and of ensuring the political independence and territorial integrity of its member states. They must also be prepared to contribute to conflict prevention and to conduct non-Article 5 crisis response operations. The Alliance's forces have essential roles in fostering cooperation and understanding with NATO's Partners and other states, particularly in helping Partners to prepare for potential participation in NATO-led PfP operations. Thus they contribute to the preservation of peace, to the safeguarding of common security interests of Alliance members, and to the maintenance of the security and stability of the Euro-Atlantic area. By deterring the use of NBC weapons, they contribute to Alliance efforts aimed at preventing the proliferation of these weapons and their delivery means.

42. The achievement of the Alliance's aims depends critically on the equitable sharing of the roles, risks and responsibilities, as well as the benefits, of common defence. The presence of United States conventional and nuclear forces in Europe remains vital to the security of Europe, which is inseparably linked to that of North America. The North American Allies contribute to the Alliance through military forces available for Alliance missions, through their broader contribution to international peace and security, and through the provision of unique training facilities on the North American continent. The European Allies also make wide-ranging and substantial contributions. As the process of developing the ESDI within the Alliance progresses, the European Allies will further enhance their contribution to the common defence and to international peace and stability including through multinational formations.

43. The principle of collective effort in Alliance defence is embodied in practical arrangements that enable the Allies to enjoy the crucial political, military and resource advantages of collective defence, and prevent the renationalisation of defence policies, without depriving the Allies of their sovereignty. These arrangements also enable NATO's forces to carry out non-Article 5 crisis response operations and constitute a prerequisite for a coherent Alliance response to all possible contingencies. They are based on procedures for consultation, an integrated military structure, and on co-operation agreements. Key features include collective force planning; common funding; common operational planning; multinational formations, headquarters and command arrangements; an integrated air defence system; a balance of roles and responsibilities among the Allies; the stationing and deployment of forces outside home territory when required; arrangements, including planning, for crisis management and reinforcement; common standards and procedures for equipment, training and logistics; joint and combined doctrines and exercises when appropriate; and infrastructure, armaments and logistics cooperation. The inclusion of NATO's Partners in such arrangements or the development of similar ar-

rangements for them, in appropriate areas, is also instrumental in enhancing cooperation and common efforts in Euro-Atlantic security matters.

44. Multinational funding, including through the Military Budget and the NATO Security Investment Programme, will continue to play an important role in acquiring and maintaining necessary assets and capabilities. The management of resources should be guided by the military requirements of the Alliance as they evolve.

45. The Alliance supports the further development of the ESDI within the Alliance, including by being prepared to make available assets and capabilities for operations under the political control and strategic direction either of the WEU or as otherwise agreed.

46. To protect peace and to prevent war or any kind of coercion, the Alliance will maintain for the foreseeable future an appropriate mix of nuclear and conventional forces based in Europe and kept up to date where necessary, although at a minimum sufficient level. Taking into account the diversity of risks with which the Alliance could be faced, it must maintain the forces necessary to ensure credible deterrence and to provide a wide range of conventional response options. But the Alliance's conventional forces alone cannot ensure credible deterrence. Nuclear weapons make a unique contribution in rendering the risks of aggression against the Alliance incalculable and unacceptable. Thus, they remain essential to preserve peace.

The Alliance's Force Posture

The Missions of Alliance Military Forces

47. The primary role of Alliance military forces is to protect peace and to guarantee the territorial integrity, political independence and security of member states. The Alliance's forces must therefore be able to deter and defend effectively, to maintain or restore the territorial integrity of Allied nations and—in case of conflict—to terminate war rapidly by making an aggressor reconsider his decision, cease his attack and withdraw. NATO forces must maintain the ability to provide for collective defence while conducting effective non-Article 5 crisis response operations.

48. The maintenance of the security and stability of the Euro-Atlantic area is of key importance. An important aim of the Alliance and its forces is to keep risks at a distance by dealing with potential crises at an early stage. In the event of crises which jeopardise Euro-Atlantic stability and could affect the security of Alliance members, the Alliance's military forces may be called upon to conduct crisis response operations. They may also be called upon to contribute to the preservation of international peace and security by conducting operations in support of other international organisations, complementing and reinforcing political actions within a broad approach to security.

49. In contributing to the management of crises through military operations, the Alliance's forces will have to deal with a complex and diverse range of actors, risks, situations and demands, including humanitarian emergencies. Some non-Article 5 crisis response operations may be as demanding as some collective defence missions. Well-trained and well-equipped forces at adequate levels of readiness and in sufficient strength to meet the full range of contingencies as well as the appropriate support structures, planning tools and command and control capabilities are essential in providing efficient military contributions. The Alliance should also be prepared to support, on the basis of separable but not separate capabilities, operations under the political control and strategic direction either of the WEU or as otherwise agreed. The potential participation of Partners and other non-NATO nations in NATO-led operations as well as possible operations with Russia would be further valuable elements of NATO's contribution to managing crises that affect Euro-Atlantic security.

50. Alliance military forces also contribute to promoting stability throughout the Euro-Atlantic area by their participation in military-to-military contacts and in other cooperation activities and exercises under the Partnership for Peace as well as those organised to deepen NATO's relationships with Russia, Ukraine and the Mediterranean Dialogue countries. They contribute to stability and understanding by participating in confidence-building activities, including those which enhance transparency and improve communication; as well as in verification of arms control agreements and in humanitarian de-mining. Key areas of consultation and cooperation could include inter alia: training and exercises, interoperability, civil-military relations, concept and doctrine development, defence planning, crisis management, proliferation issues, armaments cooperation as well as participation in operational planning and operations.

Guidelines for the Alliance's Force Posture

51. To implement the Alliance's fundamental security tasks and the principles of its strategy, the forces of the Alliance must continue to be adapted to meet the requirements of the full range of Alliance missions effectively and to respond to future challenges. The posture of Allies' forces, building on the strengths of different national defence structures, will conform to the guidelines developed in the following paragraphs.

52. The size, readiness, availability and deployment of the Alliance's military forces will reflect its commitment to collective defence and to conduct crisis response operations, sometimes at short notice, distant from their home stations, including beyond the Allies' territory. The characteristics of the Alliance's forces will also reflect the provisions of relevant arms control agreements. Alliance forces must be adequate in strength and capabilities to deter and counter aggression against any Ally. They must be

interoperable and have appropriate doctrines and technologies. They must be held at the required readiness and deployability, and be capable of military success in a wide range of complex joint and combined operations, which may also include Partners and other non-NATO nations.

53. This means in particular:

a. that the overall size of the Allies' forces will be kept at the lowest levels consistent with the requirements of collective defence and other Alliance missions; they will be held at appropriate and graduated readiness;

b. that the peacetime geographical distribution of forces will ensure a sufficient military presence throughout the territory of the Alliance, including the stationing and deployment of forces outside home territory and waters and forward deployment of forces when and where necessary. Regional and, in particular, geostrategic considerations within the Alliance will have to be taken into account, as instabilities on NATO's periphery could lead to crises or conflicts requiring an Alliance military response, potentially with short warning times;

c. that NATO's command structure will be able to undertake command and control of the full range of the Alliance's military missions including through the use of deployable combined and joint HQs, in particular CJTF headquarters, to command and control multinational and multiservice forces. It will also be able to support operations under the political control and strategic direction either of the WEU or as otherwise agreed, thereby contributing to the development of the ESDI within the Alliance, and to conduct NATO-led non-Article 5 crisis response operations in which Partners and other countries may participate;

d. that overall, the Alliance will, in both the near and long term and for the full range of its missions, require essential operational capabilities such as an effective engagement capability; deployability and mobility; survivability of forces and infrastructure; and sustainability, incorporating logistics and force rotation. To develop these capabilities to their full potential for multinational operations, interoperability, including human factors, the use of appropriate advanced technology, the maintenance of information superiority in military operations, and highly qualified personnel with a broad spectrum of skills will be important. Sufficient capabilities in the areas of command, control and communications as well as intelligence and surveillance will serve as necessary force multipliers;

e. that at any time a limited but militarily significant proportion of ground, air and sea forces will be able to react as rapidly as necessary to a wide range of eventualities, including a short-notice attack on any Ally. Greater numbers of force elements will be available at appropriate levels of readiness to sustain prolonged operations, whether within or beyond Alliance territory, including through rotation of deployed forces. Taken together, these forces must also be of sufficient quality, quantity and readiness to contribute to deterrence and to defend against limited attacks on the Alliance;

f. that the Alliance must be able to build up larger forces, both in response to any fundamental changes in the security environment and for limited requirements, by reinforcement, by mobilising reserves, or by reconstituting forces when necessary. This ability must be in proportion to potential threats to Alliance security, including potential long-term developments. It must take into account the possibility of substantial improvements in the readiness and capabilities of military forces on the periphery of the Alliance. Capabilities for timely reinforcement and resupply both within and from Europe and North America will remain of critical importance, with a resulting need for a high degree of deployability, mobility and flexibility;

g. that appropriate force structures and procedures, including those that would provide an ability to build up, deploy and draw down forces quickly and selectively, are necessary to permit measured, flexible and timely responses in order to reduce and defuse tensions. These arrangements must be exercised regularly in peacetime;

h. that the Alliance's defence posture must have the capability to address appropriately and effectively the risks associated with the proliferation of NBC weapons and their means of delivery, which also pose a potential threat to the Allies' populations, territory, and forces. A balanced mix of forces, response capabilities and strengthened defences is needed;

i. that the Alliance's forces and infrastructure must be protected against terrorist attacks.

Characteristics of Conventional Forces

54. It is essential that the Allies' military forces have a credible ability to fulfil the full range of Alliance missions. This requirement has implications for force structures, force and equipment levels; readiness, availability, and sustainability; training and exercises; deployment and employment options; and force build-up and mobilisation capabilities. The aim should be to achieve an optimum balance between high readiness forces capable of beginning rapidly, and immediately as necessary, collective defence or non-Article 5 crisis response operations; forces at different levels of lower readiness to provide the bulk of those required for collective defence, for rotation of forces to sustain crisis response operations, or for further reinforcement of a particular region; and a longer-term build-up and augmentation capability for the worst case—but very remote—scenario of large scale operations for collective defence. A substantial proportion of Alliance forces will be capable of performing more than one of these roles.

55. Alliance forces will be structured to reflect the multinational and joint nature of Alliance missions. Essential tasks will include controlling, protecting, and defending territory; ensuring the unimpeded use of sea, air, and land lines of communication; sea control and protecting the deployment of the Alliance's sea-based deterrent; conducting independent and combined air operations; ensuring a secure air environment and effective extended air defence; surveillance, intelligence, reconnaissance and electronic warfare; strategic lift; and providing effective and flexible command and control facilities, including deployable combined and joint headquarters.

56. The Alliance's defence posture against the risks and potential threats of the proliferation of NBC weapons and their means of delivery must continue to be improved, including through work on missile defences. As NATO forces may be called upon to operate beyond NATO's borders, capabilities for dealing with proliferation risks must be flexible, mobile, rapidly deployable and sustainable. Doctrines, planning, and training and exercise policies must also prepare the Alliance to deter and defend against the use of NBC weapons. The aim in doing so will be to further reduce operational vulnerabilities of NATO military forces while maintaining their flexibility and effectiveness despite the presence, threat or use of NBC weapons.

57. Alliance strategy does not include a chemical or biological warfare capability. The Allies support universal adherence to the relevant disarmament regimes. But, even if further progress with respect to banning chemical and biological weapons can be achieved, defensive precautions will remain essential.

58. Given reduced overall force levels and constrained resources, the ability to work closely together will remain vital for achieving the Alliance's missions. The Alliance's collective defence arrangements in which, for those concerned, the integrated military structure plays the key role, are essential in this regard. The various strands of NATO's defence planning need to be effectively coordinated at all levels in order to ensure the preparedness of the forces and supporting structures to carry out the full spectrum of their roles. Exchanges of information among the Allies about their force plans contribute to securing the availability of the capabilities needed for the execution of these roles. Consultations in case of important changes in national defence plans also remain of key importance. Cooperation in the development of new operational concepts will be essential for responding to evolving security challenges. The detailed practical arrangements that have been developed as part of the ESDI within the Alliance contribute to close allied co-operation without unnecessary duplication of assets and capabilities.

59. To be able to respond flexibly to possible contingencies and to permit the effective conduct of Alliance missions, the Alliance requires sufficient logistics capabilities, including transport capacities, medical support and

stocks to deploy and sustain all types of forces effectively. Standardisation will foster cooperation and cost-effectiveness in providing logistic support to allied forces. Mounting and sustaining operations outside the Allies' territory, where there may be little or no host-nation support, will pose special logistical challenges. The ability to build-up larger, adequately equipped and trained forces, in a timely manner and to a level able to fulfil the full range of Alliance missions, will also make an essential contribution to crisis management and defence. This will include the ability to reinforce any area at risk and to establish a multinational presence when and where this is needed. Forces of various kinds and at various levels of readiness will be capable of flexible employment in both intra-European and transatlantic reinforcement. This will require control of lines of communication, and appropriate support and exercise arrangements.

60. The interaction between Alliance forces and the civil environment (both governmental and non-governmental) in which they operate is crucial to the success of operations. Civil-military cooperation is interdependent: military means are increasingly requested to assist civil authorities; at the same time civil support to military operations is important for logistics, communications, medical support, and public affairs. Cooperation between the Alliance's military and civil bodies will accordingly remain essential.

61. The Alliance's ability to accomplish the full range of its missions will rely increasingly on multinational forces, complementing national commitments to NATO for the Allies concerned. Such forces, which are applicable to the full range of Alliance missions, demonstrate the Alliance's resolve to maintain a credible collective defence; enhance Alliance cohesion; and reinforce the transatlantic partnership and strengthen the ESDI within the Alliance. Multinational forces, particularly those capable of deploying rapidly for collective defence or for non-Article 5 crisis response operations, reinforce solidarity. They can also provide a way of deploying more capable formations than might be available purely nationally, thus helping to make more efficient use of scarce defence resources. This may include a highly integrated, multinational approach to specific tasks and functions, an approach which underlies the implementation of the CJTF concept. For peace support operations, effective multinational formations and other arrangements involving Partners will be valuable. In order to exploit fully the potential offered by multinational formations, improving interoperability, inter alia through sufficient training and exercises, is of the highest importance.

Characteristics of Nuclear Forces

62. The fundamental purpose of the nuclear forces of the Allies is political: to preserve peace and prevent coercion and any kind of war. They will continue to fulfil an essential role by ensuring uncertainty in the mind of

any aggressor about the nature of the Allies' response to military aggression. They demonstrate that aggression of any kind is not a rational option. The supreme guarantee of the security of the Allies is provided by the strategic nuclear forces of the Alliance, particularly those of the United States; the independent nuclear forces of the United Kingdom and France, which have a deterrent role of their own, contribute to the overall deterrence and security of the Allies.

63. A credible Alliance nuclear posture and the demonstration of Alliance solidarity and common commitment to war prevention continue to require widespread participation by European Allies involved in collective defence planning in nuclear roles, in peacetime basing of nuclear forces on their territory and in command, control and consultation arrangements. Nuclear forces based in Europe and committed to NATO provide an essential political and military link between the European and the North American members of the Alliance. The Alliance will therefore maintain adequate nuclear forces in Europe. These forces need to have the necessary characteristics and appropriate flexibility and survivability, to be perceived as a credible and effective element of the Allies' strategy in preventing war. They will be maintained at the minimum level sufficient to preserve peace and stability.

64. The Allies concerned consider that, with the radical changes in the security situation, including reduced conventional force levels in Europe and increased reaction times, NATO's ability to defuse a crisis through diplomatic and other means or, should it be necessary, to mount a successful conventional defence has significantly improved. The circumstances in which any use of nuclear weapons might have to be contemplated by them are therefore extremely remote. Since 1991, therefore, the Allies have taken a series of steps which reflect the post-Cold War security environment. These include a dramatic reduction of the types and numbers of NATO's sub-strategic forces including the elimination of all nuclear artillery and ground-launched short-range nuclear missiles; a significant relaxation of the readiness criteria for nuclear-roled forces; and the termination of standing peacetime nuclear contingency plans. NATO's nuclear forces no longer target any country. Nonetheless, NATO will maintain, at the minimum level consistent with the prevailing security environment, adequate sub-strategic forces based in Europe which will provide an essential link with strategic nuclear forces, reinforcing the transatlantic link. These will consist of dual capable aircraft and a small number of United Kingdom Trident warheads. Sub-strategic nuclear weapons will, however, not be deployed in normal circumstances on surface vessels and attack submarines.

PART V: CONCLUSION

65. As the North Atlantic Alliance enters its sixth decade, it must be ready to meet the challenges and opportunities of a new century. The Stra-

tegic Concept reaffirms the enduring purpose of the Alliance and sets out its fundamental security tasks. It enables a transformed NATO to contribute to the evolving security environment, supporting security and stability with the strength of its shared commitment to democracy and the peaceful resolution of disputes. The Strategic Concept will govern the Alliance's security and defence policy, its operational concepts, its conventional and nuclear force posture and its collective defence arrangements, and will be kept under review in the light of the evolving security environment. In an uncertain world the need for effective defence remains, but in reaffirming this commitment the Alliance will also continue making full use of every opportunity to help build an undivided continent by promoting and fostering the vision of a Europe whole and free.

Appendix B

Istanbul Summit Declaration

1. We, the Heads of State or Government of the participating States of the OSCE, have assembled in Istanbul on the eve of the twenty-first century and of the twenty-fifth anniversary of the Helsinki Final Act. Since we last met we have transformed the OSCE to meet unprecedented challenges. When we met in Lisbon, the first large-scale OSCE field operation had just been established, in Bosnia and Herzegovina. During the three intervening years, we have increased dramatically the number and size of our field operations. Our common institutions have grown in number and in the level of their activities. The OSCE has expanded the scale and substance of its efforts. This has greatly strengthened the OSCE's contribution to security and co-operation across the OSCE area. We pay special tribute to the women and men whose dedication and hard work have made the Organization's achievements possible.

2. Today, we adopted a Charter for European Security in order to strengthen security and stability in our region and improve the operational capabilities of our Organization. We task the OSCE Permanent Council to take the necessary decisions to implement promptly the new steps agreed upon in this Charter. We need the contribution of a strengthened OSCE to meet the risks and challenges facing the OSCE area, to improve human security and thereby to make a difference in the life of the individual, which is the aim of all our efforts. We reiterate unreservedly our commitment to respect human rights and fundamental freedoms and to abstain from any form of discrimination. We also reiterate our respect for international hu-

manitarian law. We pledge our commitment to intensify efforts to prevent conflicts in the OSCE area, and when they occur to resolve them peacefully. We will work closely with other international organizations and institutions on the basis of the Platform for Co-operative Security, which we adopted as a part of our Charter.

3. The situation in Kosovo, FRY, in particular the humanitarian situation, remains a major challenge for the OSCE. Our thoughts still go out to the large number of Kosovo Albanians and others who lost their lives, those who saw their property destroyed and the hundreds of thousands who were expelled from and abandoned their homes. Now most of these refugees have returned. As the difficult work of rehabilitation advances, remaining refugees will be able to return. The OSCE Mission in Kosovo forms an essential part of the broader United Nations Mission working under United Nations Security Council Resolution 1244. The OSCE Mission today has more than 1,400 staff members, and plays a vital role in the process of rebuilding a multi-ethnic society in Kosovo; the first class from the OSCE Police School has graduated, and the OSCE training of judicial and administrative personnel has started. The Organization assists in developing a civil society, in supporting the formation of a pluralistic political party landscape, free media and a viable NGO community. The OSCE plays a leading role in promoting and protecting human rights, and establishing respect for the rule of law. The success of this work is essential if democracy is to take root. We pledge to give it our full support. As we advance in these areas, we accelerate our work towards creating the necessary conditions for the first free elections in Kosovo, which the OSCE has been tasked to organize. We will seek to involve the local population increasingly in the efforts of the OSCE Mission.

4. Against the background of years of repression, intolerance and violence in Kosovo, the challenge is to build a multi-ethnic society on the basis of substantial autonomy respecting the sovereignty and territorial integrity of the Federal Republic of Yugoslavia, pending final settlement in accordance with UNSCR 1244. We expect this Resolution to be fully implemented and strictly adhered to by all concerned. We will assist all inhabitants of Kosovo. But they, and those who aspire to be their leaders, must work together towards a multi-ethnic society where the rights of each citizen are fully and equally respected. They must fight decisively against the cycle of hate and revenge and bring about reconciliation among all ethnic groups. Over the recent months, we have witnessed a new exodus from Kosovo, this time of Serbs and other non-Albanians. The necessary conditions must be restored so that those who have fled recently can return and enjoy their rights. Those who fought and suffered for their rights must now stand up for the equal rights of others. We firmly reject any further violence and any form of ethnic discrimination. Failure to oppose such acts will affect the security of the region.

5. The democratic shortcomings in the Federal Republic of Yugoslavia remain one of the fundamental sources of grave concern in the region. The leaders and people of the Federal Republic of Yugoslavia must put the country firmly on the path towards democracy and respect for human rights and fundamental freedoms. When conditions permit, the OSCE stands ready to assist in order to accelerate democratization, promote independent media and hold free and fair elections in the Federal Republic of Yugoslavia. We emphasize our desire to see the Federal Republic of Yugoslavia as a full partner. Real progress towards democracy will be a positive step towards equal participation of the Federal Republic of Yugoslavia in the international community, including in the OSCE, and will create a new basis for growth and prosperity.

6. We remain committed to a democratic, multi-ethnic Bosnia and Herzegovina based on the General Framework Agreement for Peace. We underline the importance of improving the functioning of common institutions, and of the continued assumption by those and other institutions of tasks undertaken by the international community. We expect Bosnia and Herzegovina to rapidly adopt the permanent election law, so that it can be implemented prior to the general elections scheduled for the autumn of 2000. We appeal to all the leaders of Bosnia and Herzegovina to take decisive steps towards bringing its two entities closer together and to create a situation where persons, goods and services can circulate freely within a single State to the benefit of stability and prosperity. We underline the importance of respect for the rule of law and of vigorous efforts to fight organized crime and corruption, which constitute a great threat to economic reform and prosperity. We remain committed to the return of refugees and internally displaced persons, in particular minority returns.

7. We underscore the importance of working with Croatian authorities to intensify efforts towards reconciliation in Croatia. The OSCE pledges to continue its assistance to a multi-ethnic Croatia through post-war confidence-building and reconciliation. We look forward to faster progress towards the return of refugees and displaced persons and the implementation of relevant international standards, particularly those related to equal treatment without regard to ethnicity, freedom of the media, and free and fair elections. The OSCE's police monitoring in the Danubian region of Croatia, which has played a valuable role in protecting the rights of individuals, demonstrates the OSCE's ability to develop new operational capabilities quickly and efficiently.

8. We reaffirm our commitment to assist Albania as it continues its social, political and economic reform process following the setbacks caused by the upheaval of 1997 and the Kosovo refugee crisis of 1999. Noting the recent progress, we call upon the Government and all political parties to improve the political atmosphere, thereby strengthening democratic institutions. We encourage the new Government of Albania to continue its fight against

crime and corruption. The OSCE is committed to continue its assistance and to work closely with the European Union and international organizations within the framework of the "Friends of Albania."

9. We commend the Government of the former Yugoslav Republic of Macedonia for its commitment to domestic reforms designed to enhance stability and economic prosperity. We reaffirm the OSCE's determination to support its efforts in this process, and emphasize the importance of continued attention to the development of inter-ethnic relations.

10. We pay tribute to the Governments and peoples of Albania and the former Yugoslav Republic of Macedonia, as most affected countries, as well as those of other neighbouring countries for their hospitality during the Kosovo refugee crisis and for their generosity in shouldering a heavy political and economic burden during this period.

11. Our experiences in South Eastern Europe demonstrate the need for a broader view of the region. We therefore welcome the adoption by the Cologne Ministerial Conference on 10 June 1999 of the Stability Pact for South-Eastern Europe, launched on the initiative of the European Union, which plays a leading role in co-operation with other participating and facilitating States, international organizations and institutions. We reinforce the message from the Sarajevo Summit: regional co-operation will serve as a catalyst for the integration of countries in the region into broader structures. The OSCE, under whose auspices the Stability Pact is placed, has a key role to play in contributing to its success, and we task the Permanent Council to develop a regional strategy to support its aims. We welcome the reports provided to us by the Special Co-ordinator for the Stability Pact and the Special Envoy of the OSCE Chairman-in-Office. The OSCE will work in close concert with our participating States and with non-governmental organizations in the region.

12. We consider that the work of the International Criminal Tribunal for the former Yugoslavia is crucial to achieving lasting peace and justice in the region, and reiterate the obligation of all to co-operate fully with the Tribunal.

13. During this year we have witnessed a significant increase in our co-operation with the five participating States in Central Asia. Political dialogue has gained from a growing number of high-level visits from the Central Asian States to the OSCE and by OSCE representatives to Central Asia. With the continuing support of our partners in Central Asia, the OSCE has now established offices in all five States. This in particular has contributed to an expansion of our co-operative activities in all OSCE dimensions. Reiterating our target of achieving comprehensive security throughout the OSCE area, we strongly welcome these positive developments. We are convinced that necessary progress in the difficult and complex transition process will be stimulated by an increase in our efforts based on co-operation and our common commitments. Strengthening the rule of law, the respect

for human rights and fundamental freedoms as well as the development of civil societies constitute one of the centrepieces in our broad framework of co-operative efforts. In this regard, we welcome the process of signing of Memoranda of Understanding between the ODIHR and the Central Asian participating States.

14. We share the concerns expressed by the participating States in Central Asia regarding international terrorism, violent extremism, organized crime and drug and arms trafficking. We agree that national, regional and joint action by the international community is necessary to cope with these threats, including those stemming from areas neighbouring the OSCE participating States. We further recognize the importance of addressing economic and environmental risks in the region, such as issues related to water resources, energy and erosion. We are convinced that strengthening regional co-operation will promote stability and security in Central Asia, and we welcome the active approach taken by the Chairman-in-Office to this effect.

15. Reaffirming our strong support for the sovereignty and territorial integrity of Georgia, we stress the need for solving the conflicts with regard to the Tskhinvali region/South Ossetia and Abkhazia, Georgia, particularly by defining the political status of these regions within Georgia. Respect for human rights and development of joint democratic institutions as well as the prompt, safe and unconditional return of refugees and internally displaced persons will contribute to peaceful settlement of these conflicts. We underscore the importance of taking concrete steps in this direction. We welcome progress reached at this Summit Meeting in the Georgian-Russian negotiations on the reduction of Russian military equipment in Georgia.

16. With regard to the Tskhinvali region/South Ossetia, Georgia, some progress has been made towards solving the conflict. We emphasize the importance of maintaining and intensifying the dialogue which is now under way. In light of further progress, we believe that an early meeting in Vienna, with participation of experts from this region, should be used to take decisive steps towards a solution. The establishment by the parties concerned of a legal framework for refugee and internally displaced persons housing and property restitution will facilitate the early return of refugees and internally displaced persons to the region. We also urge the early signing of the Georgian-Russian economic rehabilitation agreement and encourage further international economic assistance.

17. We continue to support the leading role of the United Nations in Abkhazia, Georgia. We emphasize the importance of breaking the current deadlock with regard to finding a peaceful solution to the conflict. In this respect we—and in particular those of us who belong to the Friends of the United Nations Secretary-General—are ready to work with the United Nations to prepare and submit a draft document addressing the distribution

of constitutional competencies between the central authorities of Georgia and authorities of Abkhazia, Georgia. We reiterate our strong condemnation as formulated in the Budapest and Lisbon Summit Documents, of the "ethnic cleansing" resulting in mass destruction and forcible expulsion of predominantly Georgian population in Abkhazia, Georgia, and of the violent acts in May 1998 in the Gali region. In light of the precarious situation of the returnees, we recommend that a fact-finding mission with the participation of the OSCE and the United Nations be dispatched early next year to the Gali region to assess, *inter alia,* reported cases of continued "ethnic cleansing." Such a mission would provide a basis for increased international support for the unconditional and safe return of refugees and internally displaced persons and contribute to the general stability in the area. We consider the so-called presidential elections and referendum in Abkhazia, Georgia, this year as unacceptable and illegitimate.

18. We welcome the encouraging steps which have been recently taken in the process of the settlement of the Trans-Dniestrian problem. The Summit in Kiev (July 1999) became an important event in this regard. However, there have been no tangible shifts on the major issue—defining the status of the Trans-Dniestrian region. We reaffirm that in the resolution of this problem the sovereignty and territorial integrity of the Republic of Moldova should be ensured. We stand for the continuation and deployment of the negotiation process and call on all sides and in particular the Trans-Dniestrian authorities to demonstrate the political will required to negotiate a peaceful and early elimination of the consequences of the conflict. We appreciate the continuation of the mediating efforts of the Russian Federation, Ukraine and the OSCE in the negotiation process on the future status of the Trans-Dniestrian region within the Republic of Moldova. We take note of the positive role of the joint peacekeeping forces in securing stability in the region.

19. Recalling the decisions of the Budapest and Lisbon Summits and Oslo Ministerial Meeting, we reiterate our expectation of an early, orderly and complete withdrawal of Russian troops from Moldova. In this context, we welcome the recent progress achieved in the removal and destruction of the Russian military equipment stockpiled in the Trans-Dniestrian region of Moldova and the completion of the destruction of non-transportable ammunition.

We welcome the commitment by the Russian Federation to complete withdrawal of the Russian forces from the territory of Moldova by the end of 2002. We also welcome the willingness of the Republic of Moldova and of the OSCE to facilitate this process, within their respective abilities, by the agreed deadline.

We recall that an international assessment mission is ready to be dispatched without delay to explore removal and destruction of Russian ammunition and armaments. With the purpose of securing the process of withdrawal and destruction, we will instruct the Permanent Council to consider the expansion of the mandate of the OSCE Mission to Moldova in terms of ensuring transparency of this process and co-ordination of financial and technical assistance offered to facilitate withdrawal and destruction. Furthermore, we agree to consider the establishment of a fund for voluntary international financial assistance to be administered by the OSCE.

20. We received the report of the Co-Chairmen of the OSCE Minsk Group on the evolving situation and recent developments connected with the Nagorno-Karabakh conflict and commend their efforts. We applaud in particular the intensified dialogue between the Presidents of Armenia and Azerbaijan, whose regular contacts have created opportunities to dynamize the process of finding a lasting and comprehensive solution to the problem. We firmly support this dialogue and encourage its continuation, with the hope of resuming negotiations within the OSCE Minsk Group. We also confirm that the OSCE and its Minsk Group, which remains the most appropriate format for finding a solution, stand ready to further advance the peace process and its future implementation, including by providing all necessary assistance to the parties.

21. We welcome the opening of an OSCE Office in Yerevan this year and the decision to open a similar office in Baku. These steps will enable the OSCE to strengthen our co-operation with Armenia and Azerbaijan.

22. We strongly support the work of the Advisory and Monitoring Group in Belarus, which has worked closely with the Belarusian authorities as well as with opposition parties and leaders and NGOs in promoting democratic institutions and compliance with OSCE commitments, thus facilitating a resolution of the constitutional controversy in Belarus. We emphasize that only a real political dialogue in Belarus can pave the way for free and democratic elections through which the foundations for real democracy can be developed. We would welcome early progress in this political dialogue with the OSCE participation, in close co-operation with the OSCE Parliamentary Assembly. We stress the necessity of removing all remaining obstacles to this dialogue by respecting the principles of the rule of law and the freedom of the media.

23. In connection with the recent chain of events in North Caucasus, we strongly reaffirm that we fully acknowledge the territorial integrity of the Russian Federation and condemn terrorism in all its forms. We underscore the need to respect OSCE norms. We agree that in light of the humanitarian situation in the region it is important to alleviate the hardships of the civilian population, including by creating appropriate conditions for international organizations to provide humanitarian aid. We agree that a political solution is essential, and that the assistance of the OSCE would contribute to achieving that goal. We welcome the willingness of the OSCE to assist in the renewal of a political dialogue. We welcome the agreement of the Rus-

sian Federation to a visit by the Chairman-in-Office to the region. We reaffirm the existing mandate of the OSCE Assistance Group in Chechnya. In this regard, we also welcome the willingness of the Russian Federation to facilitate these steps, which will contribute to creating conditions for stability, security, and economic prosperity in the region.

24. In a year which has seen the deployment of our largest ever mission, we have been able to welcome the successful conclusion of the work of one of our smallest, the OSCE Representative to the Joint Committee on the Skrunda Radar Station. We congratulate the parties involved in decommissioning the Radar Station on their efforts, undertaken in a spirit of constructive co-operation.

25. We welcome the successful completion of the work of the OSCE Mission to Ukraine. This work has been an important contribution by the OSCE to the process of stabilization in its Autonomous Republic of Crimea. We look forward to continued co-operation between Ukraine and the OSCE, including through the OSCE Project Co-ordinator in Ukraine, on the basis of its mandate and the Memorandum of Understanding.

26. With a large number of elections ahead of us, we are committed to these being free and fair, and in accordance with OSCE principles and commitments. This is the only way in which there can be a stable basis for democratic development. We appreciate the role of the ODIHR in assisting countries to develop electoral legislation in keeping with OSCE principles and commitments, and we agree to follow up promptly ODIHR's election assessments and recommendations. We value the work of the ODIHR and the OSCE Parliamentary Assembly—before, during and after elections—which further contributes to the democratic process. We are committed to secure the full right of persons belonging to minorities to vote and to facilitate the right of refugees to participate in elections held in their countries of origin. We pledge to ensure fair competition among candidates as well as parties, including through their access to the media and respect for the right of assembly.

27. We commit ourselves to ensuring the freedom of the media as a basic condition for pluralistic and democratic societies. We are deeply concerned about the exploitation of media in areas of conflict to foment hatred and ethnic tension and the use of legal restrictions and harassment to deprive citizens of free media. We underline the need to secure freedom of expression, which is an essential element of political discourse in any democracy. We support the Office of the Representative on Freedom of the Media in its efforts to promote free and independent media.

28. In the year of the 10th anniversary of the adoption of the Convention on the Rights of the Child, and putting the OSCE's Copenhagen commitments into practice, we commit ourselves to actively promote children's rights and interests, especially in conflict and post-conflict situations. We will regularly address the rights of children in the work of the OSCE, in-

cluding by organizing a special meeting dedicated to children in armed conflict during the year 2000. We will pay particular attention to the physical and psychological well-being of children involved in or affected by armed conflict.

29. The Co-ordinator of OSCE Economic and Environmental Activities should, under the authority of the Chairman-in-Office and the Secretary General and in close co-operation with the relevant OSCE field operations, develop regular reports concerning economic and environmental risks to security. These reports should include questions of promoting public awareness of the relationship between economic and environmental problems and security and the relationship between our Organization and others concerned with the promotion of economic and environmental security within the OSCE area. Such reports will be discussed by the Permanent Council.

30. We reaffirm our commitment to ensure that laws and policies fully respect the rights of persons belonging to national minorities, in particular in relation to issues affecting cultural identity. Specifically, we emphasize the requirement that laws and policies regarding the educational, linguistic and participatory rights of persons belonging to national minorities conform to applicable international standards and conventions. We also support the adoption and full implementation of comprehensive anti-discrimination legislation to promote full equality of opportunities for all. We commend the essential work of the High Commissioner on National Minorities. We reaffirm that we will increase our efforts to implement the recommendations of the High Commissioner on National Minorities.

31. We deplore violence and other manifestations of racism and discrimination against minorities, including the Roma and Sinti. We commit ourselves to ensure that laws and policies fully respect the rights of Roma and Sinti and, where necessary, to promote anti-discrimination legislation to this effect. We underline the importance of careful attention to the problems of the social exclusion of Roma and Sinti. These issues are primarily a responsibility of the participating States concerned. We emphasize the important role that the ODIHR Contact Point for Roma and Sinti issues can play in providing support. A further helpful step might be the elaboration by the Contact Point of an action plan of targeted activities, drawn up in co-operation with the High Commissioner on National Minorities and others active in this field, notably the Council of Europe.

32. In line with our commitment to ensure full equality between women and men, we look forward to an early approval and implementation of an OSCE gender action plan.

33. In the framework of our commitment to further strengthening of the operational capacities of the OSCE Secretariat, we will improve the OSCE employment conditions so that it can better compete for and retain well qualified personnel to enable the Secretariat to carry out its tasks and fulfil

its other responsibilities. We will take into account the need for geographic diversity and gender balance when recruiting personnel to OSCE institutions and field operations.

34. We note that a large number of participating States have not been able to implement the 1993 Rome Ministerial Council decision on legal capacity of the OSCE institutions and on privileges and immunities. With a view to improve this situation, a determined effort should be made to review issues related to the implementation of commitments under the 1993 Rome Ministerial decision. To this end, we task the Permanent Council, through an informal open-ended working group to draw up a report to the next Ministerial Council Meeting, including recommendations on how to improve the situation.

35. To address the challenges in the OSCE area quickly and efficiently new instruments are required. We welcome the establishment, in the Charter, of a Rapid Expert Assistance and Co-operation Teams (REACT) programme for the OSCE. We commit ourselves to make this concept fully operational at the shortest possible time. We are determined as a matter of priority to implement the decision made in the Charter. We will provide the expertise required and commit the necessary resources according to established procedures. We take note of the letter from the Secretary General to the Permanent Council concerning the rapid deployment of expertise. We request the Permanent Council and the Secretary General to establish a task force within the Conflict Prevention Centre aimed at developing the REACT programme and a budget that will enable REACT to be fully operational by 30 June 2000.

36. We task the Permanent Council and the Secretary General to implement within the same time frame, our decision in the Charter to set up an Operation Centre within the Conflict Prevention Centre, with a small core staff having expertise relevant for all kinds of OSCE operations, which can be expanded rapidly when required, and the decisions made to strengthen the Secretariat and our field operations.

37. We have in the Charter reaffirmed our commitment to the rule of law and stressed the need to combat corruption. We task the Permanent Council to examine how best to contribute to efforts to combat corruption, taking into account efforts of other organizations such as the Organization for Economic Co-operation and Development, Council of Europe and the United Nations. The results of this work will be reported to the 2000 Ministerial Meeting.

38. The fact that we are meeting in Turkey, which only recently suffered terrible earthquakes, brings home to us the major impact of natural disasters. We need to strengthen the international community's ability to respond to such events, by improving the co-ordination of the efforts of participating States, international organizations and NGOs. We task the Permanent Council to discuss this matter further.

39. We welcome the successful adaptation of the Treaty on Conventional Armed Forces in Europe. The adapted Treaty will provide a greater degree of military stability through a stricter system of limitations, increased transparency and lower levels of conventional armed forces in its area of application. We hope the States Parties will move forward expeditiously to facilitate completion of national ratification procedures, taking into account their common commitment to, and the central importance of, full and continued implementation of the Treaty and its associated documents until and following entry into force of the Agreement on Adaptation. Upon entry into force of the Agreement on Adaptation, OSCE participating States with territory in the area between the Atlantic Ocean and the Ural Mountains may apply for accession to the adapted Treaty, thereby providing an important additional contribution to European stability and security.

40. We welcome the OSCE Forum for Security Co-operation's efforts to advance security dialogue, co-operation, transparency and mutual confidence, as well as its work on the OSCE concept of comprehensive and indivisible security in accordance with its mandate of Helsinki 1992. We welcome the conclusion of the review process resulting in the adoption of the Vienna Document 1999 on confidence- and security-building measures, a key element of politico-military co-operation and stability. It improves current CSBMs and emphasizes the importance of regional co-operation. We remain fully committed to the principles contained in the Code of Conduct on politico-military aspects of security. We welcome the decision of the FSC to launch a broad and comprehensive discussion on all aspects of the problem of the spread of small arms and light weapons and to study concrete measures to deal with this issue, in order to respond to the challenge to peace and stability stemming from the excessive and destabilizing accumulation and uncontrolled spread of these weapons.

41. We note with satisfaction that the negotiations on regional stability, as foreseen under Article V of Annex 1-B of the General Framework Agreement for Peace have entered their substantive phase. A successful outcome to the on-going Article V negotiations would make a significant contribution to security and stability in the region. We urge the states participating in the Article V negotiations to aim to conclude their work by the end of 2000. We appreciate the OSCE's active role in facilitating the implementation of the Agreement on Confidence- and Security-Building Measures in Bosnia and Herzegovina and the Agreement on Sub-Regional Arms Control negotiated under Annex 1-B of the General Framework Agreement for Peace in Bosnia and Herzegovina.

42. We reaffirm the significance of the Open Skies Treaty: in this respect, convinced that trial flights are in no way a substitute for the regime of observation flights as set forth in the Treaty, we urge early completion of the process of its ratification and entry into force.

43. We note the widespread human suffering caused by anti-personnel mines and note the entry into force on 1 March 1999 of the Convention on the Prohibition of the Use, Stockpiling, Production and Transfer of Anti-Personnel Mines and on their Destruction. We also note the entry into force on 3 December 1998 of the Amended Mines Protocol to the UN Convention on Prohibitions or Restrictions on the Use of Certain Conventional Weapons which may be deemed to be Excessively Injurious or to have Indiscriminate Effects. We reaffirm our support for international co-operation in promoting global humanitarian action against anti-personnel mines, including promoting mine clearance activities, mine awareness programs, and the care, rehabilitation and social and economic reintegration of mine victims.

44. We take note of the report of the Chairman-in-Office on discussions held this year with regard to reviewing the scale and criteria for financing OSCE activities and instruct the Permanent Council to continue its discussions with a view to reaching agreement before the OSCE Ministerial Council Meeting in November/December 2000, so that this agreement can be applied after 31 December 2000, in accordance with the decision taken at the 1997 Copenhagen Ministerial Council Meeting.

45. We reconfirm the importance we attach to the relationship with our Partners for Cooperation as set out in the Charter for European Security. In light of our relationship with our Mediterranean Partners, Algeria, Egypt, Israel, Jordan, Morocco and Tunisia, we reaffirm that strengthening security and co-operation in the Mediterranean area is of major importance to the stability in the OSCE area. We therefore intend to enhance our dialogue and joint activities with them. We will furthermore strengthen our relationship with Japan and the Republic of Korea. We appreciate the contributions made by Japan to OSCE activities.

46. We express our gratitude to the High Commissioner on National Minorities, Mr. Max van der Stoel, for his willingness to continue in his position until a new High Commissioner on National Minorities has been appointed at the latest at the OSCE Ministerial Meeting in Vienna in November/December 2000.

47. The next Ministerial Council will take place in Vienna in November/December 2000, and will take a decision on the time and place of the next meeting of the Heads of State or Government of the OSCE participating States.

48. We welcome and accept the offer of Romania to exercise the function of Chairman-in-Office in 2001.

19 November 1999

NOTES

INTRODUCTION

1. Address to the North Atlantic Assembly, Madrid, October 21, 1991. Except where otherwise noted, all NATO documents can be obtained from the NATO website, www.nato.int. White House, U.S. Department of Defense, WEU, EU, and OSCE documents are available at www.pub.whitehouse.gov, www.defenselink.mil, www.weu.int, www.eurunion.org (not entirely reliable), and www.osce.org, respectively. The State Department (formerly U.S. Information Agency) *Washington File* website is www.usinfo.state.gov.

2. Secretary of Defense Caspar W. Weinberger, *Annual Report to the Congress Fiscal Year 1985* (Washington, DC: U.S. Government Printing Office [GPO], 1984), p. 28.

3. Even the CIA., although never an oracle, suggested in April 1990 that "East European events will continue to take place against a backdrop of declining relevance for the Warsaw pact and NATO." *The Future of Eastern Europe*, National Intelligence Estimate 12–90, Key Judgments (Langley, VA: Director of Central Intelligence, April 1990), p. vii. Emphasis added. Jennone Walker, a former State Department official, predicted: "On the issues that will matter most to Europeans and Americans in the next decade, NATO will be at best a bit player." "Keeping America in Europe," *Foreign Policy*, no. 46 (Summer 1991), p. 129.

4. The White House, *A National Security Strategy for a New Century*, December 1999, Web edition, p. 7.

5. Henry A. Kissinger, *Diplomacy* (New York: Touchstone published by Simon and Schuster, 1995), p. 23.

6. Speech by the secretary general at the annual session of the NATO Parliamentary Assembly, Amsterdam, November 15, 1999, *Washington File*, November

15, 1999. The last two priorities were added to the secretary general's initial articulation of October 19, 1999, in Strasbourg.

CHAPTER 1

1. Remarks at the conference on "Transforming NATO's Defense Capabilities," Norfolk, Virginia, November 13, 1998, U.S. Department of State *Washington File*, November 16, 1998.

2. "NATO in Southeast Europe—A U.S. Perspective," Wilton Park Conference, Brdo Castle, Slovenia, May 11, 2000, *Washington File*, May 11, 2000.

3. NATO Medium Term Defense Plan, July 1, 1954, *NATO Strategy Documents, 1949–1969* (NATO 1997), pp. 188, 121.

4. William S. Cohen, Secretary of Defense, *Annual Report to the President and the Congress 2000*, Web edition, Chapter 1, p. 3.

5. Ibid.

6. Admiral Guido Venturoni, "The Washington Summit Initiatives: Giving NATO the 'Tools' to Do Its Job in the Next Century," *NATO Review*, Web edition, vol. 47, no. 3 (Autumn 1999), pp. 2–3.

7. Pat Buchanan, *A Republic, Not an Empire* (New York: Regnery Press, 1999), p. 385.

8. Quoted in James Chace, *Acheson* (Cambridge, MA and London: Harvard University Press, 1998), pp. 204–205. The Brussels Treaty committed the parties to afford "all the military and other assistance in their power" to an attacked party, but the 1954 Modified Brussels Treaty creating the Western European Union (WEU) delegated military dimensions to NATO, whereas "in their power" then, as today, rings hollow without the United States.

9. Address to the North Atlantic Assembly, Barcelona, May 26, 1998.

10. *Washington File,* July 19, 1999.

11. Michael McFaul, "Getting Russia Right," *Foreign Policy,* no. 117 (Winter 1999–2000), pp.68–69.

12. *New York Times,* March 3, 2000.

13. *Balkans Security: Current and Projected Factors Affecting Regional Stability,* Briefing Report to the Chairman, Committee on Armed Services, House of Representatives, GAO/NSIAD-00–125BR (Washington, DC: U.S. General Accounting Office, April 2000), p. 8.

14. See Frank Boland, "NATO's Defence Capabilities Initiative—Preparing for Future challenges," *NATO Review,* vol. 47, no. 2 (Summer 1999).

15. Thomas-Durell Young, *Multinational Land Formations and NATO: Reforming Practices and Structures* (Carlisle Barracks, PA: Strategic Studies Institute, U.S. Army War College, 1997), p. 7.

16. *New York Times,* December 3, 1999.

17. John Deutch, Arnold Kanter, and Brent Scowcroft, "Saving NATO's Foundation," *Foreign Affairs,* vol. 78, no. 6 (November/December 1999), p. 54.

18. Address to the conference "The Future of NATO," The Royal Institute of International Affairs, London, October 7, 1999, *Washington File,* October 8, 1999.

19. *New York Times,* November 10, 1999.

20. U.S. Department of Defense, "Joint Statement on the Kosovo after Action Review," *Washington File,* October 14, 1999. Emphasis added.

21. *New York Times*, November 10, 1999.

22. *Army Link News*, November 1999.

23. Jeffrey Record, "Operation Allied Force: Yet Another Wake-Up Call for the Army?," *Parameters*, vol. 29, no. 4 (Winter 1999–2000), p. 18.

24. The motto of the U.S. 2nd Armored Division.

25. *New York Times*, March 10, 2000.

26. Testimony of The Honorable Franklin D. Kramer, assistant secretary of defense for international security affairs, to the Senate Foreign Relations Committee Subcommittee on European Affairs, March 9, 2000, *Washington File*, March 10, 2000.

27. *New York Times*, October 11, 1999.

28. Marc Rogers, "Alliance Aiming to Make 'Defence Capabilities Initiative' a Reality," *Jane's Defence Weekly* (jdw.janes.com.cgi.dw2/set.html/headline/jdw3289.html).

29. News briefing, December 1, 1999, Hamburg, *Washington File*, December 3, 1999.

30. Wesley K. Clark, "The United States and NATO: The Way Ahead," *Parameters*, vol. 29, no. 4 (Winter 1999–2000), pp. 5, 11.

31. François Heisbourg, "European Defence Takes a Leap Forward," *NATO Review*, Web edition, vol. 48, no. 1 (Summer 2000), p. 3.

32. "The U.S.-Russian Partnership," remarks at the conference "Russia: Ten Years After," organized by the Danish Ministry of Foreign Affairs, Copenhagen, November 8, 1999, *Washington File*, November 9, 1999. See Jeffrey A. Larsen, *NATO Counterproliferation Policy: A Case Study in Alliance Politics*, INSS Occasional Paper no. 17 (Colorado Springs, CO: Institute for National Security Studies, U.S. Air Force Academy, November 1997).

33. Transcript of press conference by Secretary of Defense William Cohen, NATO, December 2, 1999.

34. Karl-Heinz Kamp, "The Relevance of Nuclear Weapons in NATO," Special Issue: "NATO at Fifty," edited by Andrew Dorman and Thomas-Durell Young, *Defense Analysis*, vol. 15, no. 3 (December 1999), pp. 199–200.

35. MC 400/1, "MC Directive for Military Implementation of the Alliance's Strategic Concept," NATO CONFIDENTIAL, June 14, 1996. MC 400/1 contains "a description of the security situation and pronouncements about the military contribution to the execution of the tasks of NATO, the classified document contained basic principles which the future command and force structures would have to satisfy. . . . The most important part of the document was, however, devoted to the military contributions to Alliance roles and missions, the mission requirements and basic principles for the command force structures." The principal difference between the first and second iteration of this key planning document is that MC 400/1 replaced the earlier document's specific principal mission elements by more general principle missions areas. Rob de Wijk, *NATO on the Brink of the New Millennium: The Battle for Consensus*, Brassey's Atlantic Commentaries (London: Brassey's UK, 1997), p. 105, as well as pp. 101–106. For an unclassified description of the first iteration of this document, see ibid., pp. 40–44, *BASIC Reports on European Arms Control*, no. 20, February 19, 1992, pp. 6–7, and Ad Hoc Group on Review of NATO's Military Strategy, "Public Line to Take on Military Guidance for

the Implementation of the Alliance's New Strategic Concept," SRG (91) 59, December 10, 1991, NATO.

36. See Rafael Estrella, *After the Madrid Summit: Reform of the NATO Military Structure*, General Report of the Defense and Security Committee (Brussels: North Atlantic Assembly, 1997), particularly paragraph 8.

37. For a superb historical account, see Gregory W. Pedlow, "The Politics of NATO Command, 1950–1962," in *U.S. Military Forces in Europe: The Early Years, 1945–1970*, edited by Simon W. Duke and Wolfgang Krieger (Boulder, CO: Westview, 1993), pp. 15–42.

38. Klaus Naumann, "NATO's New Military Command Structure," *NATO Review*, vol. 26, no. 1 (Spring 1998), p. 12.

39. "Towards a NATO Summit," *IISS Strategic Comments*, vol. 2, no. 5 (November 1996).

40. *Frankfurter Allgemeine Zeitung*, August 5, 1996.

41. Anthony J. Faith, "A New Military Command Structure for NATO: But at What Expense?," "NATO at 50: Special Edition," edited by by Andrew Dorman and Thomas-Durell Young, *Defense Analysis*, vol. 15. no. 3 (December 1999), p. 271. For an analysis and critique of the new command structure, see Thomas-Durell Young, "NATO's Double Expansion and the Challenge of Reforming NATO's Military Structure," in *Europe in Change: Two Tiers or Two Speeds: NATO and the European Union Expansion*, edited by James Sperling (Manchester: Manchester University Press, 1999), pp. 103–120.

42. U.S. Information Service, *Security Issues Digest*, May 4, 1999.

43. Statement to the U.S. Senate Armed Services Committee, November 3, 1999, U.S. Mission NATO. Emphasis added.

44. Admiral Guido Venturoni, "The Washington Summit Initiatives," op. cit., p. 3. Emphasis added.

45. For an analysis of new missions and tasks for alliance forces, see Thomas-Durell Young, *Multinational Land Formations and NATO: Reforming Practices and Structures* (Carlisle Barracks, PA: Strategic Studies Institute, U.S. Army War College, 1997), pp. 11–13.

46. This point is admirably argued in David S. Yost, *NATO Transformed: The Alliance's New Roles in International Security* (Washington, DC: U.S. Institute of Peace Press, 1998), pp. 295–296.

47. See Jon Witford and Thomas-Durell Young, "Command Authorities and Multinationality in NATO: The Response of the Central Region's Armies," *Command in NATO after the Cold War: Alliance, National and Multinational Considerations*, edited by Thomas-Durell Young (Carlisle Barracks, PA: Strategic Studies Institute, U.S. Army War College, 1997), pp. 53–73. For greater details of the formations discussed here, see *Multinational Land Formations and NATO*, Appendices A through K.

48. Albeit written subtly, the frustrations of a former commander of the ARRC are evident in Michael Walker, "ARRC in Action," *NATO's Sixteen Nations*, vol. 41, no. 2 (1996), see particularly p. 44.

49. *Multinational Force command Authorities Handbook: Proceedings of the Central-Region Chiefs of Army Staff (CR-CAST)/Working Group on Command Authorities Required for a Multinational Force Commander* (Carlisle Barracks, PA: U.S. Army War College, September 1, 1995). For greater discussion of command authorities,

see Witford and Young, "Command Authorities and Multinationality in NATO," pp. 55–64.

50. See *Multinational Land Formations and NATO*, pp. 21–22.

51. MC 57/3, "Overall Organization of the Integrated NATO Forces," July 23, 1981, NATO CONFIDENTIAL.

52. An initial first effort of this type of document can be found in the Bi-NMC draft document, "NATO Task List," 1st Draft, March 13, 1997.

53. Admiral James O. Ellis, USN, Commander-in-Chief, U.S. Naval Forces, Europe; Commander, Allied Forces Southern Europe; and Commander, Joint Task Force Noble Anvil during Operation Allied Force, "A View from the Top," unclassified briefing slides, n.d.

54. The corps can be transferred (OPCOM) to the Strategic Commander Europe for both Article 5 and PSOs via the coordination agreement amongst the chiefs of defense of France and Germany and the Strategic Commander Europe. Yet, France does not participate in the NATO integrated military planning process. A copy of this agreement is available in German ("SACEUR-Abkommen") in *EUROKORPS und Europäische Einigung* (Bonn: Kunst & Kommunkation Ernst Martin, 1996), pp. 600–601.

55. "The Challenges Facing Europe and NATO and Partnership for Peace Member Countries," *Jane's Defence Weekly*, no. 8 (August 23, 2000).

56. See the excellent background and developmental account by David S. Yost, *NATO Transformed: The Alliance's New Roles in International Security* (Washington, DC: U.S. Institute of Peace Press, 1998), pp. 199–205. A slightly dated but also excellent assessment of CJTF can be found in Charles L. Barry, "The NATO CJTF Command Control Concept," in *Command in NATO after the Cold War*, pp. 29–52.

57. See Mario da Silva (Chief of Staff of the CJTF Planning Staff), "Implementing the Combined Joint Task Force Concept," *NATO Review*, vol. 46, no. 4 (Winter 1998), pp. 16–19.

58. Mario da Silva, "Combined Joint Task Force Concept," *NATO's Nations and Partners for Peace* (no. 1, 1999), p. 155.

59. General Klaus Naumann, "The Military Transformation," *NATO 50 Years On: Enlargement and Renewal* (London: Atalink, 1998), p. 21

CHAPTER 2

1. Henry A. Kissinger, secretary of state, "The Year of Europe," Address to the Associated Press Annual Luncheon, New York, April 23, 1973, *American Foreign Policy*, Third Edition (New York: Norton, 1997), pp. 103, 105.

2. John W. Holmes, "The Dumbell Won't Do," *Foreign Policy*, no. 50 (Spring 1983), p. 13.

3. Paul E. Gallis, coordinator, *Kosovo: Lessons Learned from Operation Allied Force*, CRS Report for Congress, November 19, 1999 (Washington, DC: Congressional Research Service, The Library of Congress, 1999), pp. 22, 24.

4. *New York Times*, November 7, 1999.

5. Ibid.

6. *New York Times*, December 3, 1999.

7. *New York Times*, December 10, 1999.

8. Carl Bildt, "Déjà vu in Kosovo," *Financial Times*, June 9, 1998.

9. Stockholm *Dagens Nyheter*, April 21, 1996, in Foreign Broadcast Information Service [FBIS], Western Europe, April 25, 1996.

10. Bonn Bulletin, no. 15, February 14, 1996, in FBIS, Western Europe, February 12, 1996.

11. Letter to John Borawski from Security Policy Department, UK Foreign and Commonwealth Office, October 2, 1996.

12. Address to the conference "The Future of NATO," October 7, 1999.

13. Statement to the Press, NATO HQ, December 15, 1999.

14. "Next Steps on European Security and Defense: A U.S. View," remarks at the conference "The Development of the Common European Security and Defense Policy: The Integration Project of the Next Decade," organized by the Institute for European Policy and the Representation of the European Commission in the Federal Republic of Germany," Berlin, December 17, 1999, *Washington File*, December 23, 1999.

15. "Preserving the Transatlantic Link," remarks at Wilton Park, January 20, 2000, *Washington File*, January 24, 2000.

16. "The Vision," Remarks by NATO secretary general at the conference "Défense europééne: le concept de convergence," Brussels, March 29, 2000, *Washington File*, March 29, 2000.

17. U.S. Department of Defense, *Allied Contributions to the Common Defense 1999*, March 1999, chapter 1, p. 1.

CHAPTER 3

1. "Peacekeeping, Military Intervention, and National Sovereignty in Internal Armed Conflict," *Hard Choices: Moral Dilemmas in Humanitarian Intervention*, edited by Jonathan Moore under the auspices of the International Committee of the Red Cross (Lanham, Boulder, New York, Oxford: Rowman and Littlefield, 1998), p. 58.

2. Raymond W. Copson, *The Use of Force in Civil Conflicts for Humanitarian Purposes: Prospects for the Post-Cold War Era*, CRS Report for Congress (Washington, DC: Congressional Research Service, Library of Congress, 1992), pp. 15–16.

3. *Nezavisimaya Gazeta*, May 30, 1998.

4. *New York Times*, December 24, 1999.

5. "Letter Dated 1 February 1999 from the Minister for Foreign Affairs of the Federal Republic of Yugoslavia Addressed to the President of the Security Council," annex 1 to UNSC Document S/1999/107, February 2, 1999.

6. Alexander Vershbow, "NATO-Russia: Promise of Partnership or Problems?," remarks at the Moscow State Institute for International Relations (MGIMO), October 28, 1999, *Washington File*, November 4, 1999.

7. U.S. Department of Defense, *Report to Congress: Kosovo/Operation Allied Force After-Action Report*, January 31, 2000, chapter 1, p.10.

8. Javier Solana, "NATO's Success in Kosovo," *Foreign Affairs*, vol. 78, no. 6 (November/December 1999), p. 117.

9. "Continuity, Clarity, and Constructive Change: NATO's Strategic Concept at the Start of the 21st Century," remarks at the Geneva Center for Security Policy, January 27, 2000, *Washington File*, January 31, 2000.

10. *Hansard*, March 25, 1999, pp. 617–618.

11. Speech at the Diplomatic Academy of the Ministry of Foreign Affairs, Kyiv, January 27, 2000.

12. Deputy Secretary of State Strobe Talbott, "The Balkan Question and the European Answer," The Aspen Institute, Aspen, Colorado, August 24, 1999, *Washington File*, August 25, 1999.

13. Javier Solana, "A Defining Moment for NATO: The Washington Summit Decisions and the Kosovo Crisis," *NATO Review*, vol. 47, no. 2 (Summer 1999).

14. Reuter, March 8, 1999.

15. Statement fo the U.S. Senate Armed Services Committee, November 3, 1999.

16. Address to the Marshall Center Graduation Ceremony, Germany, July 30, 1999, provided courtesy of U.S. Mission NATO.

17. *New York Times*, September 19, 1999.

18. "NATO's new security vocation," *NATO Review*, Web edition, vol. 47, no. 4 (Winter 1999), p. 2.

19. *Washington File*, June 12, 1998.

20. Statement to the Senate Armed Services Committee Hearing on the Military Implications of NATO's Strategic Concept, October 28, 1999, *Washington File*, October 28, 1999.

21. *International Herald Tribune*, June 23, 1998.

22. Kofi A. Annan, "Two Concepts of Sovereignty," *The Economist*, September 18, 1999.

23. Address to the UN General Assembly, September 21, 1999, *Washington File*, September 21, 1999.

24. Address to the Political Committee, North Atlantic Assembly, Edinburgh, November 11, 1998.

25. "NATO-Russia: Promise of Partnership or Problems," October 28, 1999.

26. *Washington File*, September 25, 1998.

27. *Washington File*, January 31, 2000.

28. "Purely internal disorders or revolutions would not be considered 'armed attacks' within the meaning of Article 5." 1949 Report of the Senate Foreign Relations Committee cited by Senator John Ashcroft, *Congressional Record*, July 9, 1998, p. S7893.

29. Peter Malanczuk, *Akehurst's Modern Introduction to International Law*, Seventh Revised Edition (New York: Vintage, 1998), p. 312.

30. *International Herald Tribune*, June 8, 1998.

31. Reuter, May 29, 1998.

32. Sean Kay, *NATO and the Future of European Security* (Oxford: Roman and Littlefield, 1998), p. 154.

33. Jesse Helms, "New Members, Not New Missions," *Wall Street Journal*, July 9, 1997.

34. Hearing on the Military Implications of NATO's Strategic Concept, U.S. Senate Armed Services Committee, October 28, 1999.

35. U.S. Department of Defense, *Report to Congress: Kosovo/Operation Allied Force After-Action Report*, January 31, 2000, pp. 3–4. Emphasis added.

36. Speech to the Annual Session of the NATO Parliamentary Assembly, November 15, 1999. Emphasis added.

37. *New York Times*, November 7, 1999.

38. *Annual Report to the Congress*, op. cit., note 4, pp. 5–6.

39. James E. Goodby and Kenneth Weisbrode, "Back to Basics: U.S. Foreign Policy for the Coming Decade," *Parameters*, vol. 30, no. 1 (Spring 2000), p. 53.

40. Statement of the U.S. European Command before the Senate Armed Services Committee, October 21, 1999, *Washington File*, October 21, 1999.

41. Ibid.

42. Ibid. To the contrary, Secretary of Defense Cohen and JCS Chairman General Shelton stated that "As early as May 1998 and through the balance of that year and into 1999, internal NATO planning explored a wide range of military options, including the use of both air and ground forces." "Joint Statement on the Kosovo After Action Review."

43. *New York Times*, March 12, 2000.

44. Ove Bring, "Should NATO Take the Lead in Formulating a Doctrine on Humanitarian Intervention?," *NATO Review*, Web edition, vol. 47, no. 3 (Autumn 1999), p. 24. UNGA Resolution 377 (V) of November 3, 1950, referred to a duty of the permanent UNSC members "to exercise restraint in the use of the veto" and declared "failure of the Security Council to discharge its responsibility . . . does not relieve Member States of their obligation or the United Nations of its responsibility under the Charter to maintain international peace and security." According to Robertson: "the UN Charter itself calls for action to be taken by the international community to respond to threats to peace and security and in response to grave humanitarian emergencies. Kosovo was both." Speech by Lord Robertson, NATO secretary general, "Law, Morality and the Use of Force," Institut de Relations Internationales et Stratégiques (IRIS), Paris, May 16, 2000. Available at www.nato.int/docu/speech/2000/s0005516a.htm.

45. See the interesting if skewed discussion in Memorandum Submitted by Professor Ian Brownlie CBE, QC, Foreign Affairs Committee, *Forth Report: Kosovo*, June 7, 2000, Appendix 2 (London: House of Commons, 2000).

46. Gallis, *Kosovo: Lessons Learned from Operation Allied Force*, p. 1.

CHAPTER 4

1. *Dead Souls* (London, New York, and Scarborough, Ontario: The New American Library, Signet Classics, 1961), p. 278.

2. *Rossiskaya Gazeta*, December 26, 1997, Foreign Broadcast Information Service, Special Supplement, SU/3114, January 1, 1998.

3. "The U.S.-Russian Partnership," November 8, 1999.

4. Interview with David Frost, BBC News, March 4, 2000.

5. Eugene V. Rostow, interview, "The Invasion of Czechoslovakia, 1968: The View from Washington," *Washington Quarterly*, vol. 2, no. 1 (Winter 1979), pp. 108–109.

6. Guido Gerosa, *Interim Report of the Sub-Committee on Eastern Europe and the Soviet Union*, Political Committee, North Atlantic Assembly, October 1991, p. 15.

7. For a brief overview, see John Borawski, *The NATO-Russia Founding Act*, Briefing Paper no. 12 (Brussels: International Security Information Service, 1997), and "If Not NATO Enlargement, What Does Russia Want?," *European Security*, vol. 5, no. 3 (Autumn 1996), and Dimitri Trenin, "Russia-NATO Relations: Time to

Pick Up the Pieces," *NATO Review*, Web edition, vol. 48, no. 1 (Spring–Summer 2000).

8. See *NATO-Ukraine Charter: First Act or Curtain Call?*, BITS Research Note 97.1 (Berlin Information Center for Transatlantic Security, July 1997), accessible at www.basicint.org/ukrchrtr.htm.

9. Sergei Rogov, "Five Challenges for Russia," www.peacemagazine. org/9709/rogov.htm. However, the author's assertion that decisions on use of force for reasons other than defense had to be taken together through the PJC, giving Russia a de facto veto also in the UNSC or OSCE. The act does not commit either party to undertake such operations only through the PJC, UNSC, or OSCE, but merely notes that Russia and NATO *can* undertake joint peacekeeping operations under UNSC mandate or OSCE authority, but that when this is done by the parties acting separately, the operation should be "consistent" with UN Charter and OSCE principles.

10. Buchanan, *A Republic, Not an Empire*, p. 17.

11. Consultative Council of the "Anti-NATO" Commission, *The Challenges to Russia and the State of its Strategic Nuclear Forces*, Memorandum no. 2, October 1997.

12. *Washington File*, November 18, 1999.

13. "Main Parameters of the Practical Participation of Russia in the Partnership for Peace Program" submitted by Russian Defense Minister Pavel Grachev to NATO on May 24–25, 1994.

14. News agency ITAR-TASS, April 27, 1999.

15. *Rossiskaya Gazeta*, December 27, 1997.

16. Cited in Miguel Herrero and José Luis Nunes, *Interim Report of the Subcommittee on the Southern Region*, North Atlantic Assembly, 1991, p. 1.

17. General Klaus Naumann, "A New NATO for a New Century," address at the Konrad Adenauer Stiftung, 1997.

18. ITAR-TASS, February 18, 1998.

19. Cornel General Nikolai Pishchev, "NATO: Myths and Reality," *Krasnaya Zvezda*, January 5, 1997.

20. Gallis, *Kosovo: Lessons Learned from Operation Allied Force*, p. 14.

21. *New York Times*, January 15, 2000.

22. *New York Times*, December 24, 1999.

23. "NATO-Russia: Promise of Partnership or Problems."

24. *International Herald Tribune*, September 11, 1998.

25. J.L. Black, *Russia Faces NATO Expansion: Bearing Gifts or Bearing Arms?* (New York: Rowman and Littlefield Publishers, 2000), p. 238.

26. Stephen J. Blank, "Russia and the Baltics in the Age of NATO Enlargement," *Parameters*, vol. 28, no. 3 (Autumn 1998), p. 53.

27. Interview with David Frost, BBC News, March 4, 2000.

28. "NATO in the 21st Century: Challenges and Opportunities," address to the 10th International Antalya Conference on Security and Cooperation," Antalya, Turkey, March 10, 2000, *Washington File*, March 10, 2000.

29. James E. Goodby, "A New European Concert: Settling Disputes in CSCE," *Arms Control Today* (January/February 1991), p. 4.

30. *The Debate on NATO Enlargement*, hearings before the Senate Committee on Foreign Relations, October 30, 1997 (Washington ,DC: U.S. GPO, 1998), p. 196.

CHAPTER 5

1. Walter Lippmann, *U.S. Foreign Policy: Shield of the Republic* (Boston: Little, Brown, 1943), pp. 9–10.

2. George F. Kennan, *The Cloud of Danger: Current Realities of American Foreign Policy* (Boston and Toronto: Little, Brown and Company, 1977), p. 148.

3. *Rossiskaya Gazeta*, December 26, 1997.

4. Address to the North Atlantic Assembly Plenary, Barcelona, May 26, 1998.

5. For the first histories of this process, see (former Congressman) Gerald B. Solomon, *The NATO Enlargement Debate, 1990–1997: Blessings of Liberty*, Washington Paper no. 174 (Westport, CT: Praeger 1998 for the Center for Strategic and International Studies, 1998), and James M. Goldgeier, *Not Whether But When: The U.S. Decision to Enlarge NATO* (Washington, DC: Brookings Institution, 1999).

6. George Bush and Brent Scowcroft, *A World Transformed* (New York: Vintage, 1998), p. 300.

7. For an overview and bibliography, see Michael M. Boll, "Superpower Diplomacy and German Unification: The Insiders' Views," *Parameters* (Winter 1996–1997).

8. Bush and Scowcroft, *A World Transformed*, p. 239.

9. Philip Zelikow, "NATO Expansion Wasn't Ruled Out," *International Herald Tribune*, July 6, 1995. See also Solomon, *The NATO Enlargement Debate*, p. 19.

10. Address to the International Institute for Strategic Studies, Annual Meeting, Brussels, September 10, 1993. His statement was made prior to a public denial by President Yeltsin that he had conceded in August 1993 to Poland's long-standing effort to join NATO, a result of what some referred to as "the vodka summit" in Warsaw.

11. Discussions at NATO, December 1993.

12. As argued by Buchanan, *A Republic, Not an Empire*, p. 4.

13. Sir David Gillmore, "Representing Britain Overseas: Post-Cold War Challenges," Royal United Service Institute *RUSI Journal* (December 1993), p. 15.

14. "The NATO Summit and the Future of European Security," statement of Honor Stephen A. Oxman, assistant secretary of state for European and Canadian affairs, before the Subcommittee on Coalition Defense, Senate Armed Services Committee, and the Subcommittee on Europe, Senate Foreign Relations Committee, February 1, 1994.

15. Cited in Solomon, *The NATO Enlargement Debate*, p. 39.

16. "Political Implications of NATO Enlargement," presentation to the NATO Defense College/North Atlantic Assembly Symposium on the Adaptation of the Alliance, Rome, April 28, 1997. NATO UNCLASSIFIED.

17. The administration appeared to contradict itself on the economic dimension. In his letters to senators of September 10, 1997, the president declared that "a failure of NATO to enlarge could undermine the business climate for the entire region." A month later, however, Secretary of State Madeleine Albright testified "there is no historical evidence of the fact that NATO provides economic benefits"—even though the Truman administration viewed the Marshall Plan and NATO as two sides of the security coin, with Article 3 of the Washington Treaty committing the members to "seek to eliminate conflict in their international economic policies and . . . encourage economic collaboration between any or all of them. *The Debate on NATO Enlargement*, p. 37. The architect of containment,

George Kennan, argued (completely unsuccessfully) when policy planning head in the State Department that NATO would work "to the detriment of economic recovery and of the necessity of seeking a peaceful solution to Europe's difficulties." Cited in Wilson D. Miscamble, *George F. Kennan and the Making of American Foreign Policy 1947–1950* (Princeton, NJ: Princeton University Press, 1992), p. 132.

18. Robert E. Hunter, "NATO in the 21st Century: A Strategic Vision," *Parameters*, vol. 28, no. 2 (Summer 1998), p. 24.

19. Joze Lenic, *Slovenia on the Way to NATO Membership*, Special Report, Political Committee, North Atlantic Assembly, May 1999, p. 5.

20. Steven Woehrel, Julie Kim, Carl Ek, *NATO Applicant States: A Status Report*, CRS Report for Congress, May 11, 1999, p. 13.

21. "Preserving the Transatlantic Link," January 20, 2000.

22. Speech at the Diplomatic Academy of the Ministry of Foreign Affairs, January 27, 2000.

23. *The Debate on NATO Enlargement*, p. 9.

24. Lithuanian government press release, November 17, 1998.

25. Tallinn BNS, April 15, 1996.

26. Cited in Jane M.O. Sharp, "British Views on NATO Enlargement," *NATO Enlargement: The National Debates over Ratification*, edited by Simon Serfaty and Stephen Cambone, NATO Academic Forum (NATO 1997).

27. *Washington File*, July 8, 1994. Emphasis added.

28. For a tentative appraisal, see *America's New Allies: Poland, Hungary and the Czech Republic in NATO*, edited by Andrew A. Michta (Seattle and London: Washington University Press, 1999).

29. Longin Pastusiak, *Poland on Its Way to NATO*, Political Committee, North Atlantic Assembly (October 1997), p. 2.

CHAPTER 6

1. "NATO-Russia Relations," Department of State TV Interactive Dialogue Program, *Washington File*, May 10, 2000.

2. "NATO and the NACC," presentation by John Kriendler, deputy assistant NATO secretary for political affairs, at the NATO Symposium "NATO: The Challenge of Change," US National Defense University, Washington, DC, April 26–27 1993. Emphasis added.

3. De Wijk, *NATO on the Brink of the New Millennium*, p. 114.

4. Martin Dahinden, "Swiss Security Policy and Partnership with NATO," *NATO Review*, Web edition, vol. 47, no. 4 (Winter 1999), p. 5.

5. See NATO website. For elaboration, see John Borawski, "Partnership for Peace 'Plus': Joint Responsibility for European Security," *Defence Analysis*, vol. 15, no. 3 (December 1999), pp. 323–332.

6. Address at Allied Forces Southern Europe, Naples, February 27, 1995.

7. For the NATO view, see Jette Nordam, "The Mediterranean Dialogue: Dispelling Misconceptions and Building Confidence," *NATO Review*, vol. 45, no. 4 (July-August 1997).

8. *Frankfurter Allgemeine Zeitung*, March 28, 1998.

9. Address to the Atlantic Treaty Organization, Strasbourg, October 19, 1999.

10. Statement of Daniel S. Hamilton, special coordinator for implementation of the Stability Pact for Southeastern Europe, U.S. Department of State, to the House Committee on International Relations, March 9, 2000, *Washington File*, March 10, 2000.

CHAPTER 7

1. This section draws from John Borawski, "Revisiting the Common European Home: A Rejoinder," *Security Dialogue*, vol. 31, no. 1 (2000). For a brief history of the security dimensions, see John Borawski, *A Better Peace: The Organization for Security and Cooperation in Europe*, Occasional Paper no. 65 (Tampere, Finland: Tampere University Press, 1996), *CSCE Helsinki Summit 1992*, North Atlantic Assembly Paper, 1992, and Piotr Switalski, *The OSCE in the European Security System: Chances and Limits* (Warsaw: Center for International Relations, Institute of Public Affairs, 1997). Valuable journals include *Helsinki Monitor*, a publication of the Netherlands Helsinki Committee and the International Helsinki Federation for Human Rights, and *OSCE Review*, published by the Finnish Committee for European Security (STETE). The OSCE Secretariat in Vienna and Prague does an excellent job of making available as much information as nations agree, but unfortunately this tends to boil down to what is agreed and not also what is proposed.

2. Department of State *Bulletin*, February 22, 1954. Reproduced in John Borawski, *From the Atlantic to the Urals: Negotiating Arms Control at the Stockholm Conference* (Washington: Pergamon-Brassey's, 1988), pp. 143–146.

3. Department of State *Bulletin*, December 13, 1954.

4. Speech to the Parliamentary Assembly of the Council of Europe, Strasbourg, May 10, 1990, *Europe: Czechoslovak View* (Prague: Institute for International Relations, 1990), p. 19. Emphasis added.

5. David Law, "The OSCE and European Security Architecture," presentation at the conference "The OSCE and Regional Security in the CIS," co-sponsored by the Friedrich Ebert Stiftung, Queen's University (Canada), and the International Center on Conflict and Negotiation (Tbilisi, Georgia), July 1–5, 1996.

6. Adam Kobieracki, "The Role and Functioning of the OSCE Chairmanship—The Polish Perspective," *Helsinki Monitor*, vol. 10, no. 4 (1999), pp. 20, 23.

7. *Rossiskaya Gazeta*, December 26, 1997.

8. *New York Times*, November 19, 1999.

9. *New York Times*, December 15, 1999.

10. *New York Times*, December 18, 1999.

11. *New York Times*, December 12, 1999.

12. Michael McFaul, "Getting Russia Right," p. 69.

13. Press release, NATO HQ, January 28, 1998.

14. As suggested in John Borawski, "On the Verge of a New Security Era," *OSCE Review*, vol. 7, no. 3 (1999), p. 8.

15. Holbrooke, *To End a War*, p. 137. "The less time I spent with the Europeans the more upset they became, but the more time I spend with them the less we accomplished" regarding Bosnia. Ibid., p. 165.

16. Ukrainian National Security and Defense Council Secretary Volodmyr Horbulin, *Interfax*, December 3, 1996. Likewise, proposals by Russia for a Security

Council-type OSCE body have not found favor, although such a grouping does in-formally exist. It should be noted that although NATO operates by consensus, in the early 1950s, NATO did have a "Standing Group" between 1949 and 1966 years comprising only France, the United Kingdom, and the United States providing strategic guidance. Likewise, German Foreign Minister Joschka Fischer stated in the OSCE Permanent Council on October 6, 1999 that the consensus rule "time and again leads to the organization's inability to act, to its self-obstruction and thus to it being unable to carry out its peace mission" (Speech by Joschka Fischer at the OSCE Permanent Council in Vienna, PC.DEL/493/ gg, October 6, 1999). He fa-vored decision making without the consent of the conflicting parties—possibly a road to nowhere, but new thinking all the same.

SELECTED BIBLIOGRAPHY

RECENT READINGS ON NATO

Balkans Security: Current and Projected Factors Affecting Regional Stability. Briefing Report to the Chairman, Committee on Armed Services, House of Representatives, GAO/NSIAD-00-125BR. Washington, DC: U.S. General Accounting Office, April 2000.

Black, J.L. *Russia Faces NATO Expansion: Bearing Gifts or Bearing Arms?* Lanham, MD: Rowman & Littlefield Publishers, 2000.

Borawski, John. "Revisiting the Common European Home." *Secuirty Dialogue* vol. 31, no. 1, March 2000, pp. 85–90.

———. *The NATO-Russia Founding Act.* ISIS Briefing Paper no. 12. Brussels: International Security Information Service, July 1997.

———. "NATO's other Special Relationship." *NATO-Ukraine Charter: First Act or Curtain Call?* BITS Research Note 97.1. Berlin: Berlin Information Center for Transatlantic Security, July 1997.

"Collateral Damage" or Unlawful Killings? Violations of the Laws of War by NATO during Operation Allied Force." Report EUR 70/18/00, Amnesty International, June 20, 2000.

Daalder, Ivo H. *Getting to Dayton: The Making of America's Bosnia Policy.* Washington, DC: Brookings Institution Press, 2000.

Daalder, Ivo H. and O'Hanlon, Michael E. *Winning Ugly: NATO's War to Save Kosovo.* Washington, DC: Brookings Institution Press, 2000.

De Wijk, Rob. *NATO on the Brink of the New Millennium: The Battle for Consensus,* Brassey's Atlantic Commentary. London: Brassey's UK, 1997.

De Wijk, Rob, Boxhoorn, Bram and Hoekstra, Niklaas, eds. *NATO after Kosovo.* Breda, the Netherlands: Royal Netherlands Military Academy, 2000.

Dorman, Andrew, and Young. Thomas-Durell, guest ed. *Defense Analysis, Special Issue: NATO at Fifty,* vol. 15, no. 3, December 1999.

Eisenhower, Susan, ed. *NATO at Fifty: Perspectives on the Future of the Atlantic Alliance.* Washington, DC: Center for Political and Strategic Studies, 1999.

Foreign Affairs Committee. *Fourth Report: Kosovo.* London: House of Commons, June 7, 2000.

Goldgeier, James M. *Not Whether but When: The U.S. Decision to Enlarge NATO.* Washington, DC: Brookings Institution Press, 1999.

Holbrooke, Richard. *To End a War.* New York: Random House, 1998.

Jenner, Peter, ed. *NATO 50 Years On: Enlargement and Renewal.* London: Atalink, 1998.

Kaplan, Lawrence S. *The Long Entanglement: NATO's First Fifty Years.* Westport, CT: Praeger Publishers, 1999.

Kay, Sean. "After Kosovo: NATO's Credibility Dilemma." *Security Dialogue,* vol. 31, no. 1, March 2000, pp. 71–84.

———. *NATO and the Future of European Security.* Lanham, MD: Rowman & Littlefield Publishers, 1998.

Kosovo/Operation Allied Force After-Action Report. Washington, DC: U.S. Department of Defense, January 31, 2000.

Lord Robertson of Port Ellen, secretary general of NATO. *Kosovo One Year On: Achievement and Challenge.* Brussels: NATO Office of Information and Press, March 21, 2000.

Mattox, Gail A., and Rachwald, Arthur, R., eds. *Enlarging NATO: The National Debates.* Boulder, CO: Lynne Rienner Publishers, 2001.

Michta, Andrew A., ed. *America's New Allies: Poland, Hungary, and the Czech Republic in NATO.* Seattle and London: Washington University Press, 1999.

Report to the Prosecutor by the Committee Established to Review the NATO Bombing Campaign Against the Federal Republic of Yugoslavia. The Hague: International Criminal Tribunal for the former Yugoslavia, June 13, 2000.

Roth, William V., Jr. *NATO in the 21st Century.* Brussels: North Atlantic Assembly, 1998.

Solomon, Gerald B. *The NATO Enlargement Debate, 1990–1997: Blessing of Liberty.* Center for Strategic and International Studies Washington Paper. Westport, CT: Praeger Publishers, 1998.

Sperling, James, ed. *Europe in Change: Two Tiers or Two Speeds? The European Security Order and the Enlargement of the European Union and NATO.* Manchester and New York: Manchester University Press, 1999.

Yost, David S. *NATO Transformed: The Alliance's New Roles in International Security.* Washington, DC: United States Institute of Peace Press, 1998.

Young, Thomas-Durell. *Multinational Land Formations and NATO: Reforming Practices and Structures.* Carlisle Barracks, PA: Strategic Studies Institute, U.S. Army War College, 1997.

Young, Thomas-Durell, ed. *Command in NATO after the Cold War: Alliance, National, and Multinational Considerations.* Carlisle Barracks, PA: Strategic Studies Institu te, U.S. Army War College, 1997.

INDEX

About the Authors

JOHN BORAWSKI was an editor of the journal *Helsinki Monitor*, formerly director of the Political Committee of the NATO Parliamentary Assembly in Brussels, Belgium, and security advisor to the Parliamentary Assembly of the Organization for Security and Cooperation in Europe.

THOMAS-DURELL YOUNG is European Program Manager at the Center for Civil-Military Relations at the U.S. Naval Postgraduate School in Monterey, California, and formerly Research Professor at the Strategic Studies Institute, U.S. Army War College, Carlisle Barracks, Pennsylvania.